Success Strategies for
Design Professionals

Positioning

". . . possessing a desired image to make it attractive to a part of the market . . ."

Rosenberg's Dictionary of Business & Management

SuperPositioning

"Organizing and managing the professional services firm so it provides excellent service to its clients, does outstanding work recognized by peers, and produces commensurate results in satisfaction and material rewards for its professionals."

The Coxe Group

Success Strategies for Design Professionals

SuperPositioning for
Architecture & Engineering Firms

Weld Coxe

Nina F. Hartung

Hugh Hochberg

Brian J. Lewis

David H. Maister

Robert F. Mattox

Peter A. Piven

McGraw-Hill Book Company

New York   St. Louis   San Francisco   Auckland   Bogotá
Hamburg   Johannesburg   London   Madrid   Mexico
Milan   Montreal   New Delhi   Panama
Paris   São Paulo   Singapore
Sydney   Tokyo   Toronto

Library of Congress Cataloging-in-Publication Data

Success strategies for design professionals.

Includes index.
1. Architectural services – Marketing –
United States.   2. Engineering services – Marketing –
United States.   3. Design services – United States –
Marketing.   I. Coxe, Weld.
NA1996.S89   1987   720'.68'8   87-2702
ISBN 0-07-013311-5

1 2 3 4 5 6 7 8 9 0   DOC/DOC   8 9 3 2 1 0 9 8 7

ISBN 0-07-013311-5

The editors for this book were Nadine M. Post and Galen H. Fleck,
the designer was Naomi Auerbach, and the production supervisor
was Thomas G. Kowalczyk. It was set in Century Schoolbook
by TC Systems.

Printed and bound by R. R. Donnelley & Sons Company.

Contents

Preface

The search for the best ways to organize and manage architecture, engineering, interior design, planning, landscape architecture, and other professional design firms has occupied more and more attention over the past generation. The goal is always simple: Find the format that will allow the firm to provide excellent service to the client, do outstanding work recognized by peers, and receive commensurate rewards in professional satisfaction and material returns. The answers, however, have not been as simple to find.

As consultants with the opportunity to analyze literally hundreds of professional design firms, we have found the search for ideal management methods challenging. Each time we've observed a format that appears to work well for some or many firms, an exception has soon appeared, contradicting what looked like a good rule to follow. For example, some firms do outstanding work organized as project teams, others are very successful with a departmentalized project structure, and still others get good results with a studio format. One of the major puzzles for observers has been finding a relation between the project delivery system used by firms (that is, "how we do our work") and how the organization itself is operated (that is, "how we structure and run the firm").

After years of study and trial and error, a model has begun to emerge that holds promise for creating some order among these issues. At the heart of this model is the recognition that although no one strategy fits all firms, there is a family of understandable principles from which almost any firm of design professionals can devise its own best strategy.

We call these the SuperPositioning principles. This book sets forth the theory, a set of master strategies derived from it, and some thoughts on how to put the principles to use.

We look forward to further learning in the years ahead from the experience of professionals who apply the principles in their own firms.

The Coxe Group

Acknowledgments

The SuperPositioning principles are the result of the career-long observations and research of the authors and some very particular contributions.

Most important has been the support over 20 years of some 600 professional design firms in architecture, engineering, interior design, landscape architecture, and planning who, as clients for management consulting services of The Coxe Group, have allowed their individual successes and problems to be examined. Their contribution is the foundation on which all the SuperPositioning principles are based.

In 1983 The Coxe Group was introduced to Dr. David H. Maister, then a professor at the Harvard Business School. David had been developing a specialty of understanding professional services organizations in law, accounting, medicine, management consulting, investment banking, and so on. On a memorable day early in 1984 in Philadelphia, his work and The Coxe Group's theories and questions came together, and a synthesis began.

In short order, the emerging theory was tested before a variety of knowledgeable audiences whose feedback was invaluable in encouraging the seeds to grow. Particular thanks are due the Professional Services Management Association for providing the first forum for discussing the concept of Practice⟷Business values, to C. Ted Bellingrath, AIA, for first noting that technology and values are a matrix and do not overlap, to the Design Professional Management Association of New York for sponsoring the first workshop at which a group of design professionals worked with the SuperPositioning matrix, and to the 200 firms that supported the conference in February 1986 in Dallas at which The Coxe Group and David Maister publicly presented the fully developed model for the first time.

Special personal thanks of all the authors are due to Marianne Green for guiding the manuscript through production.

Success Strategies for
Design Professionals

1

What Is the Best Way to Manage the Firm?

Whenever a consultant is asked by a client, "What is the best way to manage my firm?," the answer is (or should be) two words: "It depends."

Rather than being evasive, the "it depends" response is a simple reflection of the fact that, although there do exist some models of successful firm management, there is no one best way to manage an architecture or engineering firm. Whether one is considering marketing, organization, leadership style, staff development, or any other management issue, one can point to a variety of successful firms that use significantly different approaches.

What does such diversity mean? Does it mean that firm leaders have a completely free choice, or that management decisions don't matter? Some professionals have reached that conclusion. At a conference on architecture firm management, John Burgee said: "Maybe it's a subject we shouldn't be discussing. Our business is not a management business."

A great many professionals would agree that management is not their primary function, but most believe that management of their firms does matter: That a firm's ability to reach its goals (whether these are client service, financial rewards, or professional satisfaction and acclaim) depends not only on the talents of those who make up the firm but also on the way in which those talents are organized, marketed, developed, and rewarded. In a word, how they are managed.

Why then do different management approaches flourish side by side? The answer is that the marketplaces in which engineering and architecture firms compete have become increasingly complex; they are subdivided into increasingly differentiated sectors. Each market sector calls for different responses by the firms that practice in them and allows professionals with different strengths and different goals to find their own niches.

When looking for influences on management decisions, it is necessary to consider both the market for clients and the market for professional talent. Competing firms can be differentiated from each other not only by occupying different positions in the client marketplace but also by taking different approaches to competing in the people market. Just as there are firms that appeal to different types of clients, so also are there firms that appeal to different types of professional workers. Since a professional firm of architects or engineers is really selling the talent, skill, and ability of its staff, the people marketplace is as important as the marketplace for clients.

It is the forces that flow from meeting the needs of the two marketplaces that help explain the existence of identifiable *master strategies* for different types of firms. There is no point to winning in the client marketplace if the firm cannot recruit, motivate, and retain the professionals that it needs to serve its clients. Similarly, there is little value in constructing a set of firm management practices that appeal to professionals but do not result in the type of work that clients find attractive. Professional firm management is a matter of balancing the frequently conflicting needs of the two groups.

The firm's organization structure provides one opportunity to reconcile the needs of the two markets. For example, the mix of projects that the firm pursues will determine the mix of staff that is required. Looked at in another way, a firm's method of structuring career and promotion opportunities, together with its target growth rates and turnover rates, will determine the mix of talents and experience that the firm has available for client projects. Clearly, the two markets are closely connected.

Through its economic structure, a firm must reconcile the financial interests of the client marketplace (fee structure and fee levels) with the financial interest of the people market (compensation systems and levels). How the money comes into the firm is determined by the types of projects the firm undertakes and the prices it sets for its work. How the money is spent will determine the firm's ability to attract and retain personnel of different types.

Since the two marketplaces (and a firm's positioning in them) are the major determinants of the best management practices for a firm, it is worthwhile to examine some of the recent changes in the world of professionals.

Market Factors Impacting
Professional Firms

In the past, the typical engineering or architecture firm prided itself on being able to accommodate a wide range of client needs and project types. As firms or as individuals, great satisfaction was derived from the variety of work experiences provided by a generalist approach to projects.

Increasingly, however, the marketplace is pressuring firms, hence individuals, to specialize and to concentrate their practices around particular types of projects, particular types of clients, particular technical disciplines, and so on. Accordingly, many firms are facing different management challenges based on the mix of projects that they undertake.

Proliferation of service lines

A natural consequence of an increasing demand for specialists is the fact that, both within the professions as a whole and inside individual firms, there are an increasing number of subspecialties. Frequently, these subspecialties have staffing requirements, project structures, and economics very different from those of other parts of the practice, and hence they have different management needs. Accordingly, firms are faced with the problem of choosing new areas of practice with care in order to successfully integrate them into the smooth functioning of the firm.

Client sophistication

Even within well-defined areas of practice, engineering and architecture firms are facing increasingly sophisticated clients. More and more, clients have full information about the range and types of services available to them, detailed understanding of their own needs, and detailed knowledge of their professionals' costs and fee levels. Hence, they have the ability to distinguish among firms that are more or less suited to their needs. These clients are able to make informed judgments about quality and to see the trade-offs between extra cost and enhanced quality. For different projects, clients may choose to stress different selection factors: cost, quality, delivery speed, personality of the service, or any of a number of other criteria. More and more, clients are selecting their professionals on a project-by-project basis: the days of unquestioning client loyalty to one consultant seem to be over.

Greater diversity among members
of the firm

An obvious consequence of the increasing market demands for specialization is that, as individuals come to concentrate in different types of
work, the firm must organize itself to accommodate varying talents.
When all the firm's professionals are generalists, there tends to be a
more natural harmony of interests—all professionals work on the
same (broad) mix of projects and have similar work experiences and
work backgrounds. Increasingly, however, specialization requires people who have different backgrounds, work experiences, and goals. The
modern firm has the challenge of integrating and accommodating the
values of increasingly differentiated professionals.

Design technology affecting organization
of work

Increasingly, it is both possible and necessary for firms to make
greater use of work plans, systems, and procedures to deliver an end
result without each step of the work itself being invented de novo.
Work activities can (and increasingly must) be designed to capture the
qualities and economies inherent in doing work similar to that done for
previous projects. This redesign of work stages can result in the need
for more consistent procedures to process work between and among the
various staff levels of the firm.

More nonbillable staff work

Because of the continued rise in competitive intensity, more and more
firms find that they must give significant attention to a variety of firm
management tasks. These tasks include strategic planning, marketing, staff training, and financial management. Since the culture of
most professional firms is such that these managerial tasks are not as
highly valued as tasks that involve direct work on client projects, the
firm must wrestle with ensuring that they receive appropriate attention from the firm's senior professionals without distracting too much
from what is frequently referred to as "the *real* work around here."

Need for coordination

Another consequence of increasing specialization and departmentali-
zation is that the firm faces an increased need to coordinate the talents
within the firm to meet the full range of the client's need. Whereas the
individual principal in the past had a significant degree of autonomy,
today that autonomy is under attack because of the need for the firm to
engage in more collective efforts to succeed in the marketplace. If the

firm is to create an identity in the marketplaces in which it competes, everyone in the firm must contribute to creating that identity.

Short Life Cycles for Innovations

In today's marketplace, innovative breakthroughs do not remain proprietary for long. Accordingly, few firms can rest on their laurels. New techniques and approaches are constantly appearing. This evolution has a major consequence for the architecture or engineering firm: it implies that skill building, at all levels, must be a continuous process.

In all professions, junior and senior professionals are increasingly mobile; they are more prepared than ever to jump ship to advance their careers. In spite of this mobility, it is increasingly necessary for engineering and architecture firms to meet their skill needs by "making" their own skilled staff rather than by attempting to buy it on the open market. At the hiring stage, the firm acquires its raw material: recent graduates who are bright, ambitious, and talented. The firm then faces the task of turning this raw material into experienced, capable, fully developed professionals. In the long run, the success or failure of the firm will depend, to no small degree, on its ability (through a good apprenticeship and coaching system) to create and sustain the expertise that it sells.

The Test of Consistency

These trends reveal the complexity of interconnections between what is happening in the two marketplaces and the internal consequences for the firm. It is, therefore, not surprising that there is no single best way to manage an architecture or engineering firm. The philosopher who said "You can never change just one thing" was correct. A change in the mix of projects that the firm undertakes will, in most instances, have significant consequences for the mix of people that the firm requires, and that, in turn, will require that all the management mechanisms of the firm be reexamined.

The chapters that follow demonstrate the fundamental message that good management is a matter of making sure that the decisions the firm makes in one area are compatible and consistent with the decisions that it makes in all the other areas. The single greatest source of management problems inside engineering and architecture firms lies not in management choices that are poor in an absolute sense, but in inconsistency and incompatibility between the various systems of the firm.

For example, a firm might be pursuing a market that is a poor fit with the strengths of its project delivery system. Neither the target market nor the project delivery system is necessarily wrong; one is simply not appropriate to the other. One or the other must be altered. Similarly, a firm might hire people who, given its compensation and ownership system, are inappropriate; again, neither the hiring nor the system may be foolish, but together the two produce an inconsistency that is hard to manage.

Because of the need to make sure that the management decisions are mutually compatible, only a limited number of options are open to firms in designing overall management systems. There are basically six generic types which are explained in the chapters that follow. The format suggested makes it possible to identify the combination of choices that best fit the position of each professional and/or firm. The goal is to enable the reader to identify his or her own firm and test its management practices for the internal compatibility and consistency that are the key to successful architecture and engineering firms.

2

The Two Key Drivers that Shape Architecture and Engineering Firms

The concept of a set of master strategies to organize and manage architecture and engineering firms comes not from the similarities of successful firms, but from the differences.

Contrasts abound. In carrying out projects, some firms do outstanding work when organized as project teams; others are very successful with departmentalized project structures. Some design firms are very successful in serving entrepreneurial, developer clients, while others do an outstanding job working with institutions and public agencies. Frequently, each firm has difficulty working well with the other client type. Some organizations function well as partnerships with collegial decision making; others are equally comfortable with corporate formats and hierarchical chains of command. Some firms share ownership broadly with key people in the firm; others are closely held from generation to generation.

The question that has challenged observers of these contrasts in design firm strategies is this: With so many different approaches to success, how does one firm decide its best course?

In searching for a pattern of organization and management strategies to guide engineering and architecture firms, several observations stand out:

- Individual firms that have the longest records of successful achievement appear to do what they do in a fairly uniform manner. In other words, their approaches to doing work and operating the firm are clear, and these practices are followed consistently over time.

- The area in which consistency is most notably different from firm to firm—but in which consistency within a given firm seems to yield important results—is in project delivery systems, that is, how the work of the firm is done.

- In organization terms, the firms that do best tend to adopt one approach to their leadership-ownership structure and do not tamper with it from generation to generation.

As these factors are analyzed, what becomes clear is that the differences that shape most firms can be traced to two broad areas:

How a firm does its work (i.e., the process for executing projects and delivering results for the clients). This area is a firm's *design technology.*

The philosophy of the firm's professional leaders about how they will organize and operate themselves (i.e., the structure of the organization and how it is managed). This area is a firm's *organization values.*

Put another way, *design technology* shapes what the firm does best; *organization values* determine how its professionals will govern themselves and the rewards they will receive.

Recognition of these two key drivers—design technology and organization values—provides for the first time a rational basis for understanding why some firms succeed by doing things one way while others can be equally successful doing things quite differently. The new awareness also sheds some light on the reverse—why some firms never seem to find the right combination to meet all their goals.

Chapters 3 and 4 describe these two key drivers in detail and explain their influence on the course of architecture and engineering firms.

3

Design Technology—Driver of the Firm's Projects

The choice of the words "design technology" to describe how a design firm executes its projects and assignments is deliberate, even though it may be initially confusing to engineers and architects who work with other applications of the words every day.

The dictionary* defines "technology" as the "methods and materials used to achieve . . . . . objectives." Although the more familiar applications of this definition may come to mind first, it is important to understand that, in the context of an architecture or engineering firm, the definition is equally apt when applied to a firm's processes for doing its work.

Consider a land development engineering firm that places each assignment in the hands of a project manager who then leads (or follows) it through departments of surveying, planning, road and street design, utility design, and construction inspection until it is completed. This firm's master technology is its project manager–departmentalized process of doing its work. Further, within each department there will be (or should be) derivative technologies defining the process by which assignments are carried forward in each discipline. All the following are parts of the firm's design technology: the format of the plats prepared by surveying, the type of public submittals that the planning department prepares to gain local approval, who in the firm will decide whether the road and street department details curbs or grass swales, and the lettering style for making standard notations on the construc-

---

* By permission. From Webster's Third New International Dictionary © 1986 by Merriam-Webster Inc., publisher of the Merriam-Webster Dictionaries.

tion drawings. When taken together, these factors say: This is how this firm does land development work.

In contrast, consider the design technology implications of an architecture firm headed by a designer who acts as principal-in-charge of all work done by the firm. The firm assembles an ad hoc team of architects for each project; this team is expected to develop the design under the principal's leadership, produce the contract drawings and specifications, work with subconsultants in structural, mechanical, and electrical engineering, review shop drawings, and inspect construction until the project is complete. The firm's design director and project team technology is just as valid for its work as the land development engineering firm's technology is for its work.

Organizational and Operational Impacts

Once defined, however, the two firms' approaches to executing typical projects will, or should, have profound influence on a range or organizational and operational factors in the firms. One example is the levels of staff experience required for different positions. The engineer will seek specialists to work in each department; the architect will seek generalists qualified in all phases of a project. The size of the single-leader architecture firm will be limited by the principal's capacity to be personally involved in every project. The engineering firm may grow quite large if it develops or adds qualified project managers. However, if the engineering firm's design technology gives the last word on technical matters to each department head, rather than to the project manager, its growth will be constrained as soon as the busiest department head reaches capacity.

Another example of the influence of design technology is the markets the firm will be best suited to serve. An engineering firm organized as discussed above may be highly efficient at doing subdivision roads and streets for suburban developers; it is less likely to be successful in designing highways and bridges for a larger highway agency such as a state department of transportation—unless the firm has a wholly separate department with its own, different design technology.

What stands out as one examines the design technologies of different firms is the fundamental importance of being clear about the way projects are to be handled. If all the staff members in the firm know how an assignment is to be processed and what their roles are in making the project successful, it is self-evident that the firm will get better and better at what it does. Firms that take a new approach to every project, or try to do vastly dissimilar projects with a single approach, never seem to develop the kind of clear design technologies that are characteristic of the most successful firms.

This premise does not mean that every firm can, will, or should have the same design technology. The strengths of different firms derive from their different technologies. What is important is that a firm's design technology be appropriate to the type of work the firm is doing (or pursuing) and that the same design technology be followed on as many projects as possible. Then the people in the firm and the firm's clients will receive the benefits of a consistent and ever-refined approach.

At the same time, it is important to emphasize that consistency of design technology does not equate with lack of originality or innovation in design. It is essential to understand the difference between the *product* of design and the *process* of design.

The Three Primary Categories

When differences in the technologies of engineering or architecture firms are analyzed, they can be grouped into three broad areas across a spectrum:

> *Strong Delivery* design technologies provide highly efficient service on similar assignments, often to clients who seek more of a product than a service. The project technology of a Strong Delivery firm will be designed to repeat—in process and in product—the best of prior solutions over and over again with highly reliable professional quality, cost, schedule compliance, and technical excellence.

> *Strong Service* design technologies provide experienced handling of complex assignments in which the process of getting the project accomplished requires the ability to deal with conditions that may change significantly from one project to another. The project technology of a Strong Service firm emphasizes the management process that coordinates comprehensive, multidiscipline talents and services until the problem is solved or the project is built.

> *Strong Idea* design technologies provide singular expertise, innovation, or both on projects of a unique nature. The project technology of a Strong Idea firm often depends most on the working style of its leader, or guru, and it can be quite flexible according to the nature of the assignment.

Of course, every assignment in every firm has elements of delivery, service, and idea. The above distinctions are not meant to imply any lower quality in one area than in another. The successful firm will provide outstanding ideas, service, and delivery on every job. It is the extra emphasis placed on one of the three that profoundly influences how the firm can best be structured to do its projects.

Consider the implications of the three design technologies on the architectural and engineering work to design a three-story office building in a suburban location. If the client is a developer commissioning the building on speculation for multiple tenants, the project may be served best by a Strong Delivery technology provided by a firm that is a specialist in the project type and can deliver the building design reliably, efficiently, and at a very competitive fee.

In contrast, if the client is a corporation (or government agency) that expects to use the building for a regional data processing center with very complex technical support requirements, the project may best be handled by a Strong Service technology organized to program the complicated client requirements and pull together all the disciplines necessary to carry out the project. (This firm might have in-house architects and engineers.)

However, if the client is a company seeking to build a headquarters office building that will make an image statement for the organization, the project may be served best by a Strong Idea technology, in which the architectural process produces a unique solution to every project. This firm may be led by a well-known star designer.

In organization terms, the importance of the distinction is that different design technologies require very different project-handling strategies if the engineering or architecture firm is to optimize its resources.

Areas Influenced by Design Technology

Seven major areas of the firm are driven by the firm's choice of design technology:

The project-operating process

Where project decisions are made

Staffing at middle levels and below

What the firm sells

Best markets

What the firm can change

Best profit strategies

Table 3-1 illustrates how these factors may vary from one design technology to another in successful firms. The choice of one approach over another has a profound influence on the course and activities of the firm.

TABLE 3.1   Organization Characteristics of Different Technologies

Organization area	Strong Idea technology	Strong Service technology	Strong Delivery technology
1. Project operating structure	Flexible teams organized around each project	Departments, studios, or teams led by hands-on project leaders	Departments working like an assembly line or specialized teams that focus on one project type
2. Project decision making	Single authority or guru	Principal-in-charge or department head	Most decisions are standardized for each project specialty.
3. Project staffing	The best and the brightest	Train and retain experience.	Paraprofessionals
4. What the firm sells	Innovations—one-of-a-kind	"We've been there before."	Expert product
5. Best markets	Anyone with a unique problem	Institutions, public agencies, and major corporations	Developers (on all but largest, most complex projects), some sections of government agencies, and corporations
6. How to charge	Lump sum based on value	Hourly, open end	Lump sum based on bid
7. Profit strategy	Get highest-value premium.	Be good enough to get premium multiples.	Be most efficient.

Project Organization Examples

Strong Delivery project organizations are frequently highly departmentalized: projects move down the equivalent of an assembly line of specialists each of whom does pieces of the work in the most efficient and appropriate manner. Some Strong Delivery work is also very successfully done by project teams, provided the teams stay together and do the same type of project over and over again. In Strong Delivery firms the choice of who manages the project is generally less important to the client than the assurance that the process will produce another, similar result. The role of the client manager can be very important in a Strong Delivery technology. Without necessarily being deeply involved in the project, this person is the key link to the client and assures that the resources of the firm are being applied to produce the promised results.

Strong Service technologies, in contrast, depend heavily on the personal involvement of a hands-on principal-in-charge or project manager. The organization supporting this hands-on project leader may be a group of departments, a studio, or an ad hoc project team; the choice is usually governed by the professional strengths of the project leaders. The client of the Strong Service firm is deeply concerned with "who will be my engineer (or architect)." The project may require many different disciplines and technical skills, but the client wants—indeed, expects—to deal most closely with the professional who has the ability and authority to make final decisions. The project principal in a Strong Service firm will usually be 50 to 70 percent chargeable to projects as contrasted to the Strong Delivery firm's client manager, who is likely to be only 10 to 20 percent chargeable.

Strong Idea technologies derive their strength from the expertise of one or a very few recognized professional authorities or talents. In architecture this person is usually a leading designer or a project-type specialist; in engineering he or she is often a discipline guru who is recognized as the only person who can solve a particular type of problem. The project technology of the Strong Idea firm, therefore, must derive from the way this expert prefers to work.

The star may be the principal-in-charge on all the work, or the firm may have project managers and teams who review all their work with the expert for final approval before proceeding. The degree of personal interface required between the client and the firm's star can vary substantially so long as the client is assured of the stamp of approval of the key leader on all relevant decisions.

Influences on Markets and Clients

Many market segments lean toward different design technologies either because of the nature of the work or the way typical clients are organized. Commercial developers predominantly prefer Strong Delivery firms for their efficiency, speed, and price competitiveness. Strong Service technologies typically appeal to institutional and major corporate clients. Strong Idea technologies are not generally market oriented; instead, they appeal to a random variety of clients who want or need the particular expertise offered (unless the firm is a specialist in a particular project type).

Many government agency clients for both architects and engineers prefer a Strong Service technology, particularly at the federal level. But it is dangerous to generalize. Recently much local government engineering work has shifted from Strong Service firms to Strong Delivery firms as clients for routine projects have introduced price in their selection criteria and seek firms that can produce the product at lowest cost.

Pricing Variations

A major difference between the design technologies is that Strong Delivery work is product oriented and susceptible to bidding on price; Strong Service work, in contrast, is highly people-intensive and is best priced hourly. Firms that have the most difficulty in being successful with price proposals generally are offering the wrong design technology for the work.

The client who is buying a routinized Strong Delivery project will receive valid price responses from efficient, Strong Delivery firms. The firms willingly bid, do good work, and do well at it financially. Strong Service firms that try to get this work complain bitterly that they can't be competitive on price. The reason is that their design technology is different. Strong Service firms are organized to give personal, hand-holding professional service in difficult situations and simply are not organized to be as cost-efficient as Strong Delivery firms. The best pricing strategy for the Strong Service firm is to do most of its work on an hourly basis, with a higher multiplier if it is perceived to be better than its competitors.

The Strong Idea technology, on the other hand, never needs to be bid, nor should it ever be priced hourly. Strong Idea work is about innovation—doing one-of-a-kind assignments—and is best priced on its value via a lump sum or high multiple. The client who wants the one-of-a-kind result of a Strong Idea firm will pay whatever reasonable fee is asked. There is no other place to get what this firm does.

Thus, in market terms, how a firm is organized to deliver its work defines its project technologies, influences how it prices its services, and determines the markets in which it will be most successful.

Influences on Project Staffing

Within the firm, the differences in design technologies are equally important. Consider the people to be hired. If a firm seeks to maximize efficiency (delivery), it will do well to hire and train paraprofessionals who can run its computers and repeat similar details and procedures over and over again at the lowest wage cost. On the other hand, if the firm wants to maximize service, it will strive to develop career paths and benefit programs to retain its experienced senior professionals.

Strong Idea firms, in contrast, go where the fresh brains are; they hire the best and the brightest right out of advanced-degree programs.

The appeal for young staff is to learn at the feet of the master in exchange for low pay and long hours. These firms also welcome and encourage turnover after four or five years' experience in order to make room for newer talent.

Evolutionary Path

Design technologies of engineering and architecture firms often follow evolutionary paths that parallel the life cycles of the markets they serve (Figure 3.1).

When the engineering of hazardous waste disposal first became a major consulting market, the firms that won the initial assignments and set the parameters for the nationwide hazardous waste program were Strong Idea engineering firms with depth in PhDs. After the standards were established, however, most of the work to carry out the first projects was done by Strong Service firms whose role was to follow the new standards while dealing with the complex local differences in every project. Eventually some aspects of the market, such as the design of repetitive in-plant holding facilities, became routine and clients started price shopping this work, thereby allowing Strong Delivery firms to enter the market.

The health care market for architects is another example. When the great expansion in the hospital market started in the late 1960s, all the basic notions about how to plan and design new hospitals were developed by Strong Idea architects who specialized in the health care field. Once the new directions were clear, however, the Strong Idea firms were superseded by Strong Service firms because clients saw the complex expansion and retrofit of major hospitals as requiring a technology strong in its project management process. Also, whereas most of

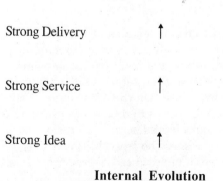

Design Technologies

Strong Delivery ↑

Strong Service ↑

Strong Idea ↑

Internal Evolution

Figure 3.1 Evolution of design technologies in the life of the firm and in the marketplace

the new ideas were generated by single-discipline architecture firms, a large share of the assignments to carry out the major projects in the health care market in the 1970s went to multidiscipline architect-engineer firms.

However, when proprietary hospital operators came into the health care market at the end of the 1970s, there was a significant shift in preferred technology. The proprietary hospital chain said in effect: "We know what an operating room is; we know what a patient room is; we need an architect simply to deliver our standard program in a local configuration." So Strong Delivery firms, organized around efficiency, quickly became the preferred providers of proprietary health care companies. Strong Service firms continued to serve the complex institutions whose programs were not adaptable to standardization. At this point in the market cycle, very little health care work was going to Strong Idea firms. The market became mature. Remember, however, that someone with a new idea might start a new cycle in the hospital market at any time.

A similar, engineering example is the Interstate Highway System. When the first Interstates were commissioned in the 1950s, there were few comprehensive federal nationwide design standards to say, for example, what radius to use for a 70-mph curve or what bridge shoulder width would assure adequate operator safety. It was a Strong Idea market, and the initial assignments went to the best and the brightest transportation engineering firms. But as soon as the standards were developed, much of the Interstate system was built by Strong Service firms.

Now the maintenance design assignments in many states are being won by Strong Delivery firms. The client is saying, "There is nothing new here. The design specifications and scope are clearly defined; we just want another 10-mile section upgraded. We don't see why we shouldn't take price proposals." However, the same client knows that if the project is a new 3-mile link through downtown Dallas, there will be no price requests. That job will go to a Strong Service firm selected primarily for its qualifications.

Internal Evolution of Design Technologies

A similar evolution often occurs inside the firm. Strong Idea markets do not often last the lifetime of their innovators, whether it be an architectural style, an engineering breakthrough, or a project-type specialization. To stay a Strong Idea firm forever, the organization must have new ideas to offer. That is not always easy, because the key people who make a firm hot when they are in their 30s and mid-40s may not generate new ideas after the original market moves on.

The founding partners have another 20 years of mileage, but they can no longer be hired for innovation alone. Such firms commonly evolve into Strong Service work and adapt their technologies to implement what they previously innovated. Many originally Strong Idea firms, in both engineering and architecture, that grew large because of their innovations in the 1960s and early 1970s today are solidly Strong Service firms.

The transition that is both most common and most difficult to make occurs when a market evolves from Strong Service to routinized Strong Delivery projects. The service firm wants gray hair and senior experience locked in, whereas the delivery firm wants efficiency from the lowest-cost people. Middle managers of Strong Service firms generally possess special education, such as a structural graduate degree, in their original design disciplines, whereas middle managers of a Strong Delivery firm are more likely to possess special graduate training in management.

It is very difficult—if not impossible—to convert Strong Service people to efficient, cost-competitive technologies. The strengths of the people are different. Thus, when a familiar service market begins to want delivery technologies, it may be best not to try to follow the market evolution but instead to enter a new market sector to which the firm's existing Strong Service technology is better suited.

Changes in Marketplace Demand

As the design technologies of individual firms evolve, evolution is also taking place in the relative demand for different types of services. Figure 3.2 illustrates the authors' collective judgment of the change over three decades in market demand for different design technologies of architecture and engineering firms. In the 1950s and 1960s the largest base of the marketplace was Strong Delivery work. The United States was still coming out of World War II; there was great demand for schools, roads, housing, and other infrastructure facilities such that quantity, not quality, was often the client's objective. Much of this work went to engineer-architects who sold volumes of work on their records of similar projects and their strengths at Strong Delivery.

An interesting change occurred in the 1970s. Clients became concerned about the lack of customized service and innovation in Strong Delivery work, and they sought more personal attention and more individual solutions. Clients wanted to know who would be the partner-in-charge, who would be the project designer, and what were his individual experience and track record. The weight of the market shifted to Strong Service firms. Strong Idea firms also multiplied somewhat in the 1970s; but although their numbers doubled, they were a small factor in the marketplace.

Design Technologies

	1960s	1970s	1980s	
Strong Delivery	50-60% ▸	35-45% ▸	35-45%	
Strong Service	40-50%	50-60%	35-45%	
Strong Idea	1-3%	3-5%	10-15%	**Figure 3.2** Changes in market demand for architecture and engineering technologies over three decades

Market Evolution

In the 1980s, a further significant shift occurred. The Strong Idea market grew very rapidly, particularly in architecture, but there are signs that engineering clients also are tiring of old solutions and are beginning to support Strong Idea engineers in some mature markets. All this shift in market has come from the share of the Strong Service firms that dominated the preceding decade.

Concurrently, the types and variety of clients seeking Strong Delivery also has expanded. This has put Strong Service firms in a double squeeze. Perhaps 80 percent of all architecture and engineering firms entering the 1980s saw themselves as Strong Service firms and organized their design technology accordingly. But only about 40 percent of the clients in the 1980s marketplace want Strong Service technology. Thus, in the mid-1980s, Strong Idea and Strong Delivery firms are thriving while Strong Service firms are hurting.

Strong Service architecture firms have tried to respond to this shift in design technology either by bringing in new design directors (Idea) or by computerizing in an effort to become more efficient (Delivery). Neither approach is working well. The most successful design directors say they do not like to work in a Strong Service structure. It is a different culture, and many designers are not comfortable in management-dominated systems. Similarly, the computers that are paying off handsomely for Strong Delivery firms are barely returning their investments in many Strong Service firms. The people operating these computers are uncomfortable becoming assembly line specialists and are too highly paid.

The same cultural issues are causing problems in Strong Service engineering firms in which the project managers and the department heads are in control of the technology. When such firms hire PhDs to bring in new ideas, the PhDs quickly want to decide for the client what will be done. The PhD says: "Let me run it!" The organization says: "The department head who hired you and the project manager will decide whether we show the client what you just decided." This sort of technology clash can be wrenching for firms. While it is underway, service inevitably suffers, and the clients may go elsewhere to have their work done.

Impact of the Last Word

A key factor in shaping a firm's design technology is the firm's philosophy about who will control project decision making—that is who will have the last word on professional matters. An engineering firm in which the project manager processes the work but key department heads have the last words on technical decisions will be a very different place from a firm in which the project manager is also project engineer and personally makes the professional and technical decisions.

The same thing is true of architects in the choice of who in the project structure will make the final design decisions. There is no magic way to know which choice is better; but once the choice is made, many other aspects of the project process will be shaped by the decision. The professional who holds the final authority over project decisions is the client's architect or engineer. That person, by the nature of this responsibility, will consequently carry pivotal weight in many aspects of both project and firm operations. *More than any other factor, where the firm elects to place the last word is the deciding element in shaping the rest of its design technology.*

It is important to recognize that these examples are not absolutes—many successful firms may do things somewhat differently or in a hybrid manner. However, analysis of the most successful architecture and engineering firms demonstrates that there is a correlation between consistency of design technologies and success and satisfaction. Chapters 6 and 7 give more comprehensive examples of how to fit different technologies into a firm's overall strategy.

4

Organization Values—
Driver of the
Firm's Professionals

There is a cartoon that has become something of a classic among young architects as they embark on what is often considered to be one of the less-remunerative professions. In the cartoon, one architect asks another: "What would you do if you inherited a million dollars?" Replies the peer: "I'd continue practicing until it was all gone."

Bruce Henderson, widely recognized management consultant and founder of the very successful Boston Consulting Group, sees management consulting as a paradoxical business. The paradox, he says, is that the professional service organization is essentially unmanageable.

In different ways, both the cartoon and the observation address common points. There is increasing evidence that the management of professional services firms is not subject to all the same principles that appear to apply to product-oriented businesses.

The number of firms of architects and engineers (plus lawyers, accountants, medical practitioners, and the like) has been increasing since the mid-1960s. Some professions are more advanced than others in applying principles of business management to their organizations, but the firms that have moved down the road are reporting frustrating difficulties.

Despite major advances in management information systems, many firms have not yet found effective mechanisms for central control. Despite important strides in professionals' understanding of marketing and project management systems, many clients for professional services continue to insist on being sold and served personally by the leaders of the professional firms, which leaves little time for those leaders to tend to the organization itself.

When the role of chief executive does exist in professional firms, it is in frequent conflict with the refusal of many key professionals within firms to submit to authority. More often than not, multiprincipal professional services firms operate as partnerships. Most decisions are made by consensus, and governance, if there is any, is provided by a management committee that facilitates rather than controls.

Perhaps most illustrative of the difficulty in applying business standards to professional services firms is the general lack of success that publicly traded organizations have had with the numerous acquisitions of engineering and architecture firms in the late 1960s and early 1970s. Not one of the publicly acquired firms has achieved significant internal growth since acquisition; many have been sold back or taken private; and virtually all have spawned very successful private competition while in public hands.

Fundamental Differences

These above experiences raise this question: Are engineering and architecture organizations really subject to the same management principles as conventional businesses are, or, in fact, are there fundamental differences? For a decade, management "authorities" have been writing article after article for both the professional and business press telling design professionals that they need to be more businesslike to survive in today's economy. Yet when professional service firms that have applied business principles to the fullest are examined, few cases that confirm the conventional premise of what being "businesslike" implies can be found.

In fact, for every engineering or architecture organization that is doing well under full application of business management, there are probably ten times as many firms doing as well or better by operating under a rather different set of rules—or no rules at all.

It is the premise of this chapter that patterns that are evident suggest there are distinct categories of professional design firms and that each category requires quite different management techniques. Professionals and managers who understand the categorical differences will be in a better position to choose the effective management approach for their firms.

The fundamental differences become evident if one examines the word "practice," which is so often used by professionals to describe their organizations, and the word "business."

Practice is "the carrying on or exercise of a profession or occupation . . . . . as a way of life."

Business, on the other hand, is "a commercial or mercantile activity customarily engaged in as a means of livelihood."*

When the two definitions are compared from a management perspective, what stands out is the contrast between "a way of life" and "a means of livelihood." In this light it is possible to see why an architect might spend an inheritance in order to carry on the profession or a noted business consultant might find some professionals unmanageable.

What is becoming evident is that many architecture and engineering firms are "practices" first and "businesses" second, and therein lies a whole new perspective about what goes on in such organizations. The contrast can be expressed as a continuum with business-centered professional firms at one end and practice-centered firms at the other as shown in Figure 4.1. Although every professional design firm on the continuum combines aspects of both business and practice, there is an enormous difference depending on which value dominates.

Architects and engineers who "practice" typically have as a major goal the opportunity to pursue their disciplines by serving others by designing their buildings or structures, planning infrastructure, solving environmental problems, or whatever. Practices often resist the doctrines of strategic planning. They are led not by their leaders, but by their clients: The work dictates the nature of the firm and what the firm does from day to day. When a client asks for a new service, the firm will change to respond, not vice versa.

Practices frequently have very unstructured—albeit very effective—programs for marketing, and they pay widely varying attention to human resources and financial issues. Some very famous firms barely break even and pay their owners little more than a living, and some make enormous amounts of money—both in a very "unbusinesslike" way.

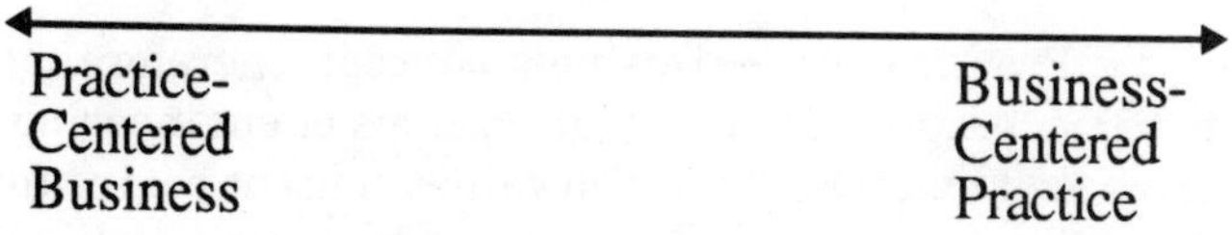

Practice-
Centered
Business

Business-
Centered
Practice

Figure 4.1 Continuum of professional firm values

---

* By permission. From Webster's Third New International dictionary © 1986 by Merriam-Webster Inc., publisher of the Merriam-Webster® Dictionaries.

The Two Bottom Lines

The essence of the differences between practice-centered and business-centered engineering and architecture firms is in their values. The values of a practice-centered organization are first professional: "What will be done, for whom, and how well?" The primary rewards are personal satisfaction in the doing and in seeing the result—a constructed project or a pleased client. The values of a business-centered design organization tend to be more tangible: "What material rewards will we receive from doing what we do?" The bottom line in a business-centered professional practice is usually *quantitative* and comparable to the bottom line of conventional business (i.e., "How well did we do on the project?"). The bottom line of a practice-centered professional firm is essentially *qualitative* (i.e., "How do we feel about how the project came out?").

It must be emphasized that there is nothing noble about either choice—even though many practicing professionals will argue differently. The choice of whether to be a practice-centered or business-centered architecture or engineering firm is an entirely selfish one; it is derived from how professionals view their missions in life and what they hope to receive from their efforts. A business-centered firm can provide service of just as high a quality to its clients as a practice-centered firm can, although the clients each serves best may be very different.

Similarly, practice-centered professional firms can make just as much money as business-centered firms can, although they may go about making their money in different ways. The same self-serving motives that govern the basic approach to practice versus business explain why some design firm practices do very well financially while others are content to barely get by as they overserve (or undercharge) their clients in order to do the work to their own satisfaction. The fundamental difference is not how well one or the other is managed; it is what their values are.

Differences between Professions

The importance of the Practice←——→Business concept, therefore, is in how it allows us to understand the many gradations of engineering and architecture firms that exist. Further, the values concept begins to explain why whole professions tend to be more or less businesslike, depending on where the majority of their members cluster on the continuum. Figure 4.2 gives a largely subjective appraisal compiled by the authors to illustrate where the different professions are positioned.

Some of the contrasts between professions are particularly reveal-

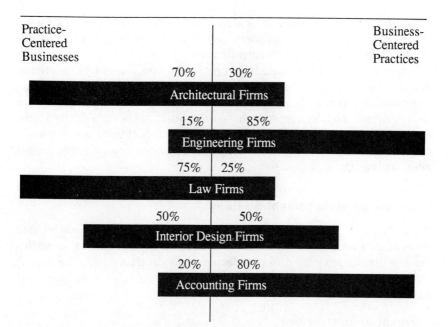

Figure 4.2 How different professions group on the continuum

ing. Architects, for example, are observed to be predominantly practice-centered, whereas consulting engineers tend to be more business-centered. On analysis it is apparent that architects are much more involved in unique, one-of-a-kind assignments that depend on intuitive, creative, and judgmental skills, whereas consulting engineering work is highly governed by prescribed standards, codes, and other procedures that encourage rational, cognitive skills and careful compliance rather than innovation.

Similarly, it can be said that lawyers, with some notable exceptions, are somewhat more practice-centered than accountants. The majority of corporate and complex personal law involves a high degree of custom service and tends to appeal to lawyers who prefer to work in practice-centered models. Accounting firms, on the other hand, work largely within the prescribed rules of the Financial Accounting Standards Board. In general, accountants tend to operate in business-based models.

All this suggests that practice values may be more attractive to professionals who have higher potential for ego rewards from more creative endeavors. Business-centered values appeal to professionals whose work is more proscribed and who measure their rewards more quantitatively. That perhaps explains why the architecture divisions of many major consulting engineering firms often have experienced difficulty coexisting within the structures of their more business-centered parents and why engineers are often frustrated working within the environment of architecture firms.

Interior design professionals can be found over the entire spectrum. Within the field itself there are vast differences between, say, contract interior firms (those that sell furniture with their designs) and pure design firms. The former are extremely business-oriented; the latter are more frequently practice-oriented. The different nature of the work and the different values of the people attracted to the two approaches may explain the difference.

Influence on Management Strategy

What is most important about the Practice←——→Business values concept is that the management of a successful engineering or architecture firm takes very different forms depending on where the firm is positioned on the continuum. The choice of values in a professional design firm directly influences these factors:

Organization structure

Organization decision-making process

How to plan

How to market

Best clients

Staffing strategy at the top

Profit strategy

Leadership and management style

Potential rewards

In each of these areas the management strategies for practice-centered firms can be quite different from the approach to managing a business-centered firm, as is illustrated in Table 4.1.

Differences in Governance

The core differences are generally determined by how best to structure and govern the organizations. Business-centered firms tend to respond well to a corporate-type organization with hierarchical command in the hands of a few controlling owners. The most useful function of management in these firms is to concentrate on fine-tuning the operation of the professional process to maximize efficiency and return to the owners.

The leadership focuses more on maintaining and building the entity

TABLE 4.1 Characteristics of Different Organization Values

Management area	Strategy	
	Practice-Centered Business	Business-Centered Practice
1. Organization structure	Proprietorship or partnership with equal ownership among peers	Corporate organization Control closely held
2. Decision-making process	Consensus decisions	Hierarchical authority
3. How to plan	Follow opportunities. Welcome new challenges. Do little formal planning.	Planned goals and objectives
4. How to market	Broad, participative marketing; home of the closer-doer	Marketing is centrally directed. Marketing representatives are used to find leads. "Closers" hand most work to different "doers."
5. Best clients	Clients who want to be personally involved with the professional who is serving them, especially institutions and entrepreneurs (developers)	Mega-corporations and government; clients who delegate the work within their organizations
6. Staffing strategy	Recruit career-oriented professionals; promote from within. Low turnover; retain maximum experience.	Hire experienced staff on a project basis. Higher turnover; tenure only for core specialists.
7. Profit strategy	Maximize rates by giving most value.	Seek lump sum fees. Maximize efficiency.
8. Leadership-management style	Focus on the professional quality of projects and long-term professional trends.	Focus on administration of the firm; attention to details; short interval results.
9. Potential rewards	Qualitative ("How did the project come out?")	Quantitative ("How did we do on the project?")

rather than on what the leaders are doing professionally. Thus, shifts in the marketplace can be taken in stride because the firm is more likely to shed divisions and services that have become unproductive and hire new key people or acquire smaller firms to help it enter new markets. The key to making all this happen is to keep control closely held in the hands of people who value the continuity and survival of the entity above what they may be doing professionally.

Practice-centered firms are most frequently proprietorships or partnerships (or corporations run like partnerships) in which principals are heavily involved in projects and the work being done drives the organization. Authority is seldom delegated, and management is most frequently by consensus. Practice-centered firms do best when their leaders are professionals with a clear commitment to and distinction in the kind of service they are offering. Being the best at what they do brings them plenty of work by reputation and referral. Staff are attracted by the nature of the assignments and will stay as long as there are interesting projects.

Administering the practice-centered firm is usually the most difficult task because the principals are disinclined to pay attention to details like wage and salary administration and monitoring project budgets but at the same time are reluctant to delegate authority over those matters to anyone else. The best solution is to employ a highly communicative administrator who enjoys facilitating decisions by the principals without requiring a stake in which way the decisions go.

Difficulties with Change

As long as the practice is growing or stable, all goes relatively well in the practice-centered professional design firm. It is when things go badly—a market turns down or dries up or a key producer retires—that the management of the practice-centered firm is frequently at a loss. In such cases an objective management observer can point without hesitation to the strategic actions that would address the problem; it always boils down not to what the principals or partners *should* do, but to what they *will* do.

Decisions about what a practice-based firm will do invariably flow from how the principals see their profession and their personal places in it. That perception is why such firms can and sometimes do lose a million dollars staying with a dying market. When a practice-centered firm finds itself in such straits, the better solution is to take a hard look at the professional strengths of the partners and slim down the firm to fit what is left of the market.

Only if the practitioners themselves are willing to work learning new tricks is it realistic to expect to remake a practice. That transformation is not always easy when, as an example, the practicing architect is philosophically opposed to postmodern design or the principal highway engineer has genuine questions about the financial viability of rapid transit.

Another hazard for practice-centered firms is to become focused on business strategies when all the professional leaders are fully involved in serving clients and leading projects. Efforts in such firms to plan growth, open branches and so on, inevitably falter because not enough leadership energy is given to tending the store. The converse is a major hazard of business-centered firms: the leaders can become preoccupied with organization strategies and lose sight of the need to carefully watch project performance and quality.

Business-centered professional service firms often get in trouble if controlling ownership is spread too broadly because, as more professionals get onto the board or management committee, conflicts over business versus practice values inevitably arise.

The Perilous Extremes

Because the Practice←——→Business concept is a continuum, there are obviously gradations of positions in which some hybridization of management strategies will work. But it is very important not to go to extremes. One of the problems of many architecture or engineering firms is that, whenever they try to rationalize an extreme position for themselves, there is a price to be paid that prevents the firm from achieving real success.

Figure 4.3 illustrates some of the extremes. At the practice end of the continuum it is possible—and not uncommon—to have a firm that might be termed a Practice-Centered Practice. Its values are so interlinked with the way of life of its professionals that it simply ignores the fundamental necessities of any business such as accountability to the clients and staff and fiscal responsibility. Examples are the engineer who is chronically late and misses critical deadlines and the architect who designs far beyond the client's budget and/or spends all the fee before construction has been adequately supervised.

In such firms staff turnover is usually excessive, there are few repeat clients, and the principals themselves seldom achieve the goals toward which their egos drive them. As the wise managing partner of a creative planning firm recently observed: "If you are a Practice-Centered Practice, you are really out of business!" That is true in more ways than one.

At the opposite end of the continuum is a very different, but similarly unrealistic, professional design organization: the business-centered business. This is the limb on which publicly held conglomerates found themselves when they bought a flock of engineering and architecture firms in the early and middle 1970s.

Practice- Centered Practice	**Practice- Centered Business**	Organization- Centered Organization	**Business- Centered Practice**	Business- Centered Business
(Out of Business)		(Out of Service)		(Out of Professionals)

Figure 4.3 Perilous extremes of the Practice ←——→ Business spectrum

What happens most often at this extreme of the continuum is that the organization cannot attract or retain professionals sufficiently qualified to do the work in a satisfactory manner. The better engineers and architects realize they are the essential assets of the business-centered firm, and they know they can own it themselves if they move across the street and hang out their own shingles. At the same time, the client is smart enough to recognize qualified professional service and will not support the Business-Centered enterprise that does not embody strong professional orientation.

More common and most misleading in its appeal is the very dangerous middle of the Practice←——→Business continuum. In terms of values, the closer one gets to the center of the continuum, the more business values tend to be replaced by *organization* values.

> *Organization,* as defined in the dictionary, is "a group of people that has a more or less constant membership . . ."*

Firms too close to the center of the continuum frequently exhibit values that concentrate on preserving their people without regard to the quality or marketability of whatever services they are offering. They become Organization-Centered Organizations.

An example could be an architecture-engineering firm that developed a top-heavy departmental structure in a period when it had huge projects overseas and is now trying to serve smaller domestic projects and clients without changing the service organization. While younger, more flexible firms offer clients a menu of choices, the entrenched values of the Organization-Centered Organization will too long retain the obsolete service structure and thereby turn off both new clients and younger, enthusiastic staff.

Professional design firms that have just experienced transition of ownership frequently fall into that position. The entrepreneurs who founded and led the firm have retired and turned it over to their loyal deputies. The deputies complement the skills of the founders but cannot duplicate them. Rather than promote talented subordinates, or bring in new blood, they hold fast to the existing team while the firm gets deeper and deeper into trouble.

The Organization-Centered Organization exists solely to serve itself—the perfect bureaucracy in which neither practice values nor business values are strong enough to override its need to preserve itself. Clients of such organizations soon discover they are a second or

---

* By permission. From Webster's Third New International Dictionary © 1986 by Merriam-Webster Inc., publisher of the Merriam-Webster® Dictionaries.

third priority of the professionals, and so they move on to other, more service-oriented firms.

There are, of course, midpoints on the Practice←——→Business continuum at which organization values are appropriate and can be managed successfully. The point in stressing the extreme of the center is that engineering and architecture firms frequently find themselves in the dangerous position described above not by conscious choice, but by common denominator. Whenever there are conflicting values among leaders of a professional firm, any effort to compromise tends to produce a middle ground.

When all of the conflicts are on either one side or the other of the Practice←——→Business continuum, the compromise position is often a quite successful place to be. If, however, the conflict is between practice-centered professionals on one side and business-centered professionals on the other, striking a compromise will inevitably lead to preoccupation with the organization, and both the firm and its clients will suffer. This dilemma frequently occurs when different disciplines try to practice together, as in architecture and engineering firms, and the leaders of the two disciplines are not from the same end of the Practice←——→Business continuum.

How to Avoid the Pitfalls

It should now be clear that, to manage a professional services firm successfully, it is very important to understand where the principal professionals' values fall on the Practice←——→Business continuum. That position will then call for its own distinct management response.

Making that happen, however, is not as easy as it sounds. Probably the single most important management action in every professional services firm is choosing partners and/or key staff who share common values. This selection can be accomplished when organizing a new firm by having the prospective principals spend time sharing how they want to structure, control, and market the firm and what they seek as rewards. If all the principals find they are in agreement with common values, the new firm will have taken a giant step toward success— whichever end of the spectrum it chooses.

It is in established firms that are in evolution that consensus on values becomes more difficult to achieve. In the first place, the values of the founders can shift over time (and this change is perfectly acceptable if everyone shifts in the same direction). However, it is very important to know whether new key people joining the firm or moving up to partnership have the current values or different values.

Often, the successor generation represents a mixture of values. When the group is diverse and there is no consensus, the management goal must be to avoid settling for compromise. If differences are irreconcilable, the firm may be better off if it divides into several directions. This split happens all the time in architecture and engineering firms, and it can be a necessary role of management to facilitate continuing evolution as new principals come and go.

Locating the Management Role

Thus, a key to managing any professional design firm is where the management itself is vested. There was a time when it was believed that there would be a role for management-trained generalists to operate engineering and architecture firms for their members. In pursuit of that belief the Professional Services Management Association (PSMA) was organized in the 1970s by the business managers on the staffs of architecture and engineering firms. PSMA was planned as a peer group through which business-oriented managers were expected to explore and master the management of the professional organizations they served.

However, after rapid early growth, PSMA's membership peaked at about 1000 and began to decline. The majority of its present members are professional engineers and architects who wear both practitioner and manager hats in their organizations. The number of pure business managers in PSMA who hold significant management roles in professional design firms is very small.

The inescapable conclusion is that, to manage most architecture, engineering, and similar professional design firms, the professionals must learn to manage themselves. They may have management-trained assistants to administer and coordinate, but the basic management direction and policies of the firm must come from the top professionals. How they go about it will, of course, differ greatly with their choice of values.

The measure of success in the professional design firm will always be the collective bottom line of the professionals themselves. Although the bottom line can be and sometimes is measured quantitatively, it is often the qualitative values of the professionals that are the real bottom line. All management in engineering and architecture firms must begin with understanding how great that difference is.

5

The SuperPositioning Matrix

The SuperPositioning principles derive from a new view of how the key drivers described in the preceding chapters can be combined into a meaningful framework for understanding the differences in engineering, architecture, and similar professional design firms. At the heart of this framework is the recognition that, although no one strategy fits all firms, there is an understandable group of principles from which almost any firm of design professionals can find its own best strategy.

At the foundation of the SuperPositioning principles is a recognition that the relationship of the two key drivers described earlier—a firm's design technology and its organization values—can be expressed as the two axes of a matrix as in Figure 5.1.

Axis of Design Technology

The vertical axis in Figure 5.1 is made up of the three broad design technologies described earlier:

Strong Delivery technologies organized to provide highly efficient service on similar or routinized assignments, often for clients who seek more of a product than a service.

Strong Service technologies organized to deliver experienced and reliably managed services, especially on complex assignments.

Strong Idea technologies organized to deliver singular expertise or innovation on projects of a unique or one-of-a-kind nature.

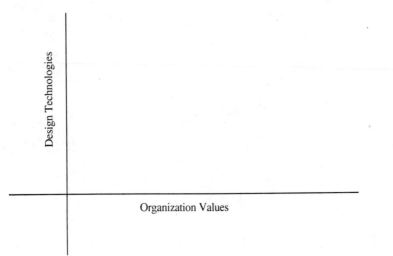

Figure 5.1   The two drivers as axes of the SuperPositioning matrix

The different technologies, when they are working best, require notably different project-operating organizations, staffing patterns, decision structures, and so on, as listed in Table 5.1.

It is important to emphasize that there is nothing judgmental about the quality of any of the three design technologies. Each technology, when it is most successful, has a vitally important component of design, service, and delivery. It is the emphasis that makes the difference.

Although it is traditional that many design professionals want their firms to be able to respond to all types of clients who need the entire range of design technologies, the SuperPositioning principles recog-

TABLE 5.1   Organization and Management Factors Driven by Choice of Technology and Values

Factors driven by design technology	Factors driven by organization values
The project operating process	Organization structure
Where project decisions are made	How organization decisions are made
Staffing at middle levels and below	How to plan
What the firm sells	How to market
Best markets	Best clients
What the firm can charge	Staffing strategy at the top
Best profit strategies	Leadership-management style potential rewards

nize that really successful firms limit their activities to what they do best and have a clear and consistent project process for doing it. This premise gives meaning to the different positions on the vertical axis of the matrix.

The tables in Chapter 6 illustrate the differences in strategies that are influenced by a firm's choice of technology.

Axis of Organization Values

The horizontal axis of the SuperPositioning matrix (Figure 5-1) is defined by the range of organization values of the professionals leading the firm. The fundamental differences in values, as described in Chapter 4, flow from the contrast between the word "practice" and the word "business." Many architecture and engineering firms are practices first and businesses second; others are businesses first and practices second. The basic difference is their bottom line:

> *Practice-Centered Businesses* are driven by professionals who typically have it as their major goal to use the discipline they represent to serve others and have a *qualitative* bottom line focused on how they feel about the work they are doing.

> *Business-Centered Practices* are driven by professionals who are more likely to have as their personal objectives a *quantitative* bottom line which is derived from the tangible rewards of their efforts.

It must be emphasized again and again that there is nothing intrinsically noble about a firm's choice of values. Either choice can produce equally successful results in client service, professional quality, and profitability. What is most important about this distinction is the recognition that, although all successful design professionals clearly strike a balance between practice values and business values, it makes a significant difference which of the two values is primary. The different positions—practice-centered versus business-centered—will lead to very different choices in significant areas of organization and management as listed in Table 5.1.

What is most valuable about the recognition of organization values as a key driver in shaping engineering and architecture firms is the importance of having all the leading professionals in the firm share similar goals. As the best organization patterns for the different values are examined, it becomes clear that any effort to compromise values will inevitably weaken some of the choices and consequently weaken the firm. Thus, just as with design technology, it is consistency of organization values that provides the foundation for the most successful strategies.

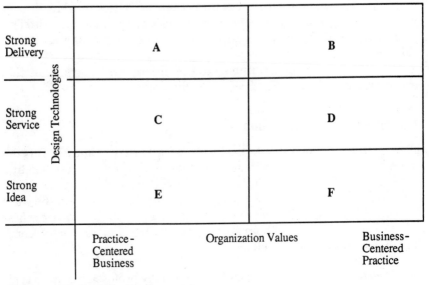

Figure 5.2   The SuperPositioning matrix

Forming the Matrix

When the two key drivers—design technology and organization values—are placed in combination, the matrix they form (Figure 5.2) defines six basic types of firms, each of which has a very different best strategy for the considerations described in Table 5.1. These various strategies, shaped by different combinations of technologies and values, produce the essence of the SuperPositioning principles for organizing and managing architecture and engineering firms. Examples of best strategies for each of the six positions are given in the following chapters.

What can be seen from the matrix, for the first time, is a clear picture of why some firms succeed by doing things one way while others are equally successful by doing things quite differently. It is also clear that it is very difficult to optimize any firm that mingles too many of the different strategies. When this recognition is combined with the understanding that the best clients and best markets for different technologies and values are distinct, it is possible to take a whole new view of how firms can best position their strengths to serve their clients and themselves.

Firms that have a clear notion of what they do best (their design technology) and have a common set of goals (their organization values) always have succeeded best—for their clients and themselves.

6

Master Strategies for Organizing and Managing by the SuperPositioning Principles

The SuperPositioning principles are based on the premise that there are distinct categories of professional design firms and for each category there is a best set of organization and management strategies which, if followed, will allow the firm to optimize its success. This chapter presents a composite set of master strategies for each position in the SuperPositioning matrix.

It is important to stress that these master strategies are not intended to establish or suggest inviolate rules. Many firms operate quite successfully in positions that are composites of more than one strategy; other firms can argue that they are significant exceptions to one or more of the general directions suggested. Obviously, there is no master approach that is absolutely guaranteed to succeed if followed, or to fail if violated.

The primary objective in presenting the strategies which follow is to illustrate the interdependence of all the organization and management choices that apply to any one position or category. The idea is to encourage firms first to focus on their own uniqueness—for example, "What position in the SuperPositioning matrix is our strong suit?"— and then determine the best strategies to follow to optimize that position. Experience with the SuperPositioning principles has demonstrated that firms with the greatest consistency in their strategies have greater success achieving their goals.

The most successful firms seek work they are best suited to do and, in general, match their organizations and management strategies to that position. The examples that follow are intended to help all firms understand the choices that have to be made and find the master strategy that is right for them.

I Master Strategies for Project Process and Decision Making

Strong Delivery	Projects are processed through departments or teams in accordance with standard details and specifications developed through experience. Partners-in-charge make any necessary decisions. Success is achieved by delivering a good product efficiently.	Projects follow an assembly line process through a departmentalized system in which established standards are critically important. Since the product is standard, the client may deal with several job captains over the course of the project. Quality control is the key to client satisfaction.
Strong Service	Projects are delivered through project teams or studios whose principals-in-charge (the closer-doers) have a high degree of involvement in project decision making. Experienced, technically oriented people provide quality-control input, but project success relies on the authority and experience of the closer-doers.	Projects are headed by project managers and delivered by departments whose department heads usually have authority over project decision making and responsibility for quality control.
Strong Idea	Creative direction originates from the idea (design) principal. Projects are delivered via highly flexible teams established and organized around jobs.	Projects are delivered via stable teams or studios that often are organized around particular client or project types. Idea principal(s) maintain project authority.
	Practice-Centered Business	Business-Centered Practice

II Master Strategies for Organization Structure and Decision Making

	Practice-Centered Business	Business-Centered Practice
Strong Delivery	This firm practices best as a proprietorship or corporation closely held by one or a few design professionals who manage a vertical organization. Decision making tends to be autocratic, and the firm thrives as long as the principals stay closely involved.	This firm is frequently "investor" owned by insiders or outsiders who delegate much of the operations and management. Decisions are largely based on standardized processes or procedures that work as long as the firm's process or product does not become obsolete.
Strong Service	This firm is broadly owned by professionals functioning as a partnership, whether legally structured as a partnership or as a corporation. Organization decision making is by consensus. It functions best when owners share similar professional capability and goals.	This firm could be a proprietorship, a closely held partnership, or a corporation with owners making decisions by majority rule. Decisions are clearly oriented toward meeting the goals of major owners.
Strong Idea	This firm is usually owned by a sole proprietor or a few equal owners who function as partners. Their ideas and creativity in projects drive the firm, and few organization decisions are made.	This firm is usually a proprietorship or small partnership (or closely held corporation functioning as a partnership). Organization decisions are tailored to maximize the application of one or a few original ideas.

III　Master Strategies for Staff Recruitment and Development

Strong Delivery	This firm recruits experienced professionals who are committed to getting the job done efficiently. Financial compensation—base and bonus—tends to be higher than the market norm. There is limited job security except at the top.	The most effective strategy for this firm is to hire and train paraprofessionals to do a maximum amount of the work via standardized procedures. The firm invests in training, not salary and benefits, to keep costs low, efficiency high, and establish an assembly line culture with compensation by job classifications and a publishable benefit package.
Strong Service	This firm recruits career-oriented professionals with a strong sense of commitment to the client. Compensation consists of security via stability of practice, good benefits, and pensions but average or below-average salary. The goal is to provide security and retain experience via low turnover.	This firm hires experienced professionals as workload requires, seeking those comfortable in a corporate-like structure. It provides higher pay and limited benefits. People at the top are entrenched; this kind of firm exhibits less loyalty to staff when workload declines.
Strong Idea	Young bright professionals are attracted to this firm by its reputation and the opportunity to be associated with one of the idea leaders (gurus) of the profession. Staff members typically receive below-market salaries and minimal benefits, and they move on after a few years unless tapped to join the inner circle.	This firm will recruit either young bright professionals interested in learning from the firm or experienced experts with records as innovators. Compensation at lower levels of staff is often below market norm—the attraction is working on interesting projects. As staff members develop experience and want higher rewards, turnover is encouraged in order to make room for new talent.
	Practice-Centered Business	Business-Centered Practice

IV   Master Strategies for Sales Message and Type of Clients

Strong Delivery	This firm sells its proven track record and the principals' knowledge and understanding of how to get through the system and agencies. The best clients are volume developers and organizations interested in reliable, proven, repeat-type solutions. Past clients return because of the firm's track record and their rapport with the principals.	This firm sells a product: a standardized design produced on an assembly line ("It will only take a moment and we'll have it all done."). Package deals are particularly popular. The best market for this firm is the one-time or repeat client unconcerned with originality and/or looking only at the bottom line.
Strong Service	This firm sells closer-doer experience, technical skills, and commitment to remain on top of the job with a personalized, tailored approach to the client. Best clients are institutions and agencies with complex projects who seek reliable solutions and expect to be involved in their projects' evolution. High repeat business is provided by well-satisfied past clients.	This firm sells its track record, demonstrably competent project managers, and the strength of the organization to back them up. Its best clients are major corporations and agencies with large projects the execution of which the client expects to delegate after making the selection.
Strong Idea	The sales message is the reputation of the guru, a track record of successful innovation, and/or solutions to uncommon problems. This firm's best clients are those with unique one-of-a-kind problems or patrons with individual or corporate egos to satisfy. Clients are always the top decision makers, and they may bypass input from their organizations.	This firm's best markets are usually clients seeking leading-edge solutions that have been successfully tested by others, e.g., developers or lower-risk corporations and institutions. They respond to the firm's reputation and "sizzle"—messages like "innovation that is cost-effective."
	Practice-Centered Business	Business-Centered Practice

v Master Strategies for Marketing Approach and Marketing Organization

Strong Delivery	Principals sell one-on-one; they may actively take opportunities to past clients. Effective advertising and public relations campaigns keep the principals' and firm's names in front of the market. Marketing staff supports those efforts.	Marketing is carefully planned and managed. Sales representatives find and sometimes close leads. Bidding opportunities are welcomed. Advertising promotes a standard product or service. This kind of firm often relies on heavy entertainment of prospects and blanket coverage of conventions.
Strong Service	Marketing depends on closer-doer principals who are strong at finding and courting clients. A facilitative marketing manager (who may be a principal) encourages broad staff participation in marketing. This firm produces a high-quality brochure, a client newsletter, and articles in both professional and user-oriented publications. It seeks to have a good record of awards and recognition by professional or user groups.	Marketing and sales are centralized under a strong marketing director who is responsible for preparing the marketing plan. The firm will employ bird dogs or prospectors to find leads and will use targeted direct mail, client seminars, and some advertising. Sales are closed by one or a few principals who hand off work to project managers.
Strong Idea	Marketing is generally unplanned. This firm relies almost entirely on a reputation developed via books, articles, professional society awards, entry in premier design competitions (often invited), frequent speeches, and often a faculty appointment. Marketing staff, if any, maintains photographic and written project information for responding to inquiries.	Marketing is actively planned, particularly in efforts to get to know specific clients, to seek publicity and publication of articles in leading magazines, to produce effective brochures, and so on. A marketing coordinator keeps the program moving.
	Practice-Centered Business	Business-Centered Practice

VI Master Strategies for Pricing and Profit

Strong Delivery	This firm specializes in producing a relatively standard product over and over again. It does best by charging lump-sum fees—since it profits from efficiency. Maximizing efficiency—reducing the costs of production—increases profits.	This firm's assembly line process for delivering a standardized product thrives on volume. Thus, the firm can bid low to keep volume up. Lump-sum or per unit fees are essential.
Strong Service	Given the choice, this firm prices all its work hourly; it produces steady cash flow with moderate but assured profits. Even if time-and-materials contracts are not possible, it establishes its fees based on hours and costs of service. Asking for (and being worth) a higher multiplier increases profits.	To maximize return, this firm focuses only on profitable activities; it minimizes nonbillable time, carefully controls overhead, and maximizes multipliers. This firm can do well on lump-sum fees, hourly rates, or costs plus fixed fees.
Strong Idea	Economically, this firm does best if it bases fees on the value—not the cost—of what it delivers by charging either higher rates and multiples or high lump sums.	This firm strives to capitalize monetarily on the innovative ideas it develops via value-added premiums, royalties, and the like.
	Practice-Centered Business	Business-Centered Practice

VII Master Strategies for Leadership and Management

Strong Delivery	An authoritative owner (or group of owners) leads the firm; it establishes an environment that attracts professionals willing to subordinate themselves to, and implement, defined management policies.	Owners delegate operational authority to managers who structure rigid processes to keep the assembly line working.
Strong Service	In its optimum configuration, this firm has broadly based ownership with many equals. It can thrive on weak leadership as long as all are committed to the goals. Consistent organization management is provided best by a facilitative general manager.	Owners assign strong management authority to a chief executive officer who is likely to be the most influential among them (or the majority owner).
Strong Idea	Strong leadership values preclude the need for structured management. The firm is led by its projects, and it relies on administrative support to take care of necessary organization tasks.	This firm's strong leadership is based on the ability to draw ideas and creativity from others. Management is a coordinating and administrative function.
	Practice-Centered Business	Business-Centered Practice

VIII Rewards to the Principals

	Practice-Centered Business	Business-Centered Practice
Strong Delivery	This firm produces high professional esteem for the principals from its clients as well as high monetary rewards.	This firm produces high monetary rewards for the principals by maximizing volume in a specialty.
Strong Service	Rewards in this firm relate to security for many in the firm—both professionally and financially in terms of benefits and growth to ownership.	This business-oriented service firm rewards the few at the top with high monetary returns.
Strong Idea	The essential reward for this kind of firm is fame in the marketplace. Wide recognition of the importance of the ideas brings new opportunities.	This firm seeks monetary rewards as well as fame. It will not consider itself successful unless it makes money as well as builds a reputation.

Composite Strategies
for the Six Positions

The following are composite master strategies for firms in each type of sector in the SuperPositioning matrix. The composites are not intended to be either typical or representative of any firm that might occupy a particular position. Rather, they simply illustrate how the SuperPositioning principles interact.

In reviewing these composites, design professionals must make allowance for the cultural characteristics that differentiate various disciplines.

Architects, for example, are generally more practice-centered and therefore tend to reflect more of the practice-type strategies even when operating in a business-centered value model.

Consulting engineers are more likely to combine Strong Service and Strong Delivery technologies and will often do so within divisionalized business-centered organizations.

Interpro engineers, whose clients are other design professionals (usually architects), frequently reflect the design technology models of their clients. Interpros with business-centered values, however, often modify their structures to relate to practice-centered clients; yet at the same time they seek assignments as prime consultants so their fees can be higher.

Interior design firms often separate themselves on the values axis between those who provide contract services (combining design and furnishings sales) and those who offer exclusively professional design services. The former tend to prefer business-centered models, while the latter most often follow practice-centered models.

Land surveying firms tend to operate in Strong Delivery business-centered models, and they frequently have difficulty integrating other consulting engineering services with the organization unless the areas are clearly divisionalized.

Landscape architecture firms often divide in two directions depending on whether they sell plant materials (business-centered models) and on whether they offer site planning and urban design services. The latter usually involve two very different technologies (Strong Delivery and Strong Idea, respectively).

Planning firms are the most difficult of all design firms to position because they can offer so many varieties of services. The services range from land development site planning to providing regional demographic master plans. Multiservice planning firms often find they are operating in so many technologies it is difficult to choose one strategy.

The above generalizations are not made to help any firm identify its own strategy; rather, their purpose is to underline the variables that may influence a given firm's perspective on its alternatives. The objective, for all firms, is to focus attention on the merit of clearly defining one's position(s) and adopting the most appropriate strategies to optimize that position or those positions.

To supplement the following composites, see the appendixes for representative examples of how architecture, engineering, and interior design firms apply the SuperPositioning principles.

Composite Type A Firm

Strong Delivery
Practice-Centered

A	B
C	D
E	F

Project Process and
Decision Making

Projects are processed by departments or teams in accordance with standard details and specifications developed through experience. Principals-in-charge make any necessary decisions. Success is achieved by delivering a good product efficiently.

Organization
Structure and
Decision Making

This firm practices best as a proprietorship or corporation closely held by one or a few design professionals who manage a vertical organization. Decision making tends to be autocratic, and the firm thrives as long as the principals stay closely involved.

Staff Recruitment and
Development

This firm recruits experienced professionals who are committed to getting the job done efficiently. Financial compensation—base and bonus—tends to be higher than the market norm. There is limited job security except at the top.

Sales Message and
Type of Clients

This firm sells its proven track record and the principals' knowledge and understanding of how to get through the system and agencies. The best clients are volume developers and organizations interested in reliable, proven, repeat-type solutions. Past clients return because of the firm's track record and their rapport with the principals.

Marketing Approach
and Marketing
Organization

Principals sell one-on-one; they may actively take opportunities to past clients. Effective advertising and public relations campaigns keep the principals' and the firm's names in front of its market. Marketing staff supports these efforts.

Pricing and Profit Strategy

This firm specializes in producing a relatively standard product over and over again. It does best by charging lump-sum fees—since it profits from efficiency. Maximizing efficiency—reducing the costs of production—increases profits.

Leadership and Management

An authoritative owner or owners leads or lead the firm, thereby establishing an environment that attracts professionals willing to subordinate themselves to, and implement, defined management policies.

Rewards

This firm produces high professional esteem from its clients from the principals as well as high monetary rewards.

Composite Type B Firm

Strong Delivery
Business-Centered

A	B
C	D
E	F

Project Process and Decision Making

Projects follow an assembly line process through a departmentalized system in which established standards are critically important. Since the product is standard, the client may deal with several job captains or project engineers over the course of the project. Quality control is the key to client satisfaction.

Organization Structure and Decision Making

This firm is frequently "investor" owned by insiders or outsiders who delegate a great deal of the operations and management. Decisions are largely based on standardized processes or procedures that work as long as the firm's process or product does not become obsolete.

Staff Recruitment and Development

The most effective strategy for this firm is to hire and train paraprofessionals to do a maximum amount of the work via standardized procedures. The firm invests in training, not salary and benefits, to keep costs low and efficiency high and to establish an assembly line culture with compensation by job classification and a publishable benefit package.

Sales Message and Type of Clients

This firm sells a product, a standardized design, produced on an assembly line ("It will only take a moment and we'll have it all done."). Package deals are particularly popular. The best market for this firm is the one-time or repeat client unconcerned with originality and/or looking only at the bottom line.

Marketing Approach and Marketing Organization

Marketing is carefully planned and managed. Sales representatives find and sometimes close leads. Bidding opportunities are welcomed. Advertising promotes a standard product or service. This kind of firm often relies on heavy entertainment of prospects and blanket coverage of client conventions.

Pricing and Profit Strategy

This firm's assembly line process for delivering a stardardized product thrives on volume. Thus, the firm can bid low to keep volume up. Lump-sum or per-unit fees are essential.

Leadership and Management

Owners delegate operational authority to managers who structure rigid processes to keep the assembly line working.

Rewards

This firm produces high monetary rewards for the principals by maximizing volume in a specialty.

Composite Type C Firm

Strong Service Practice-Centered

A	B
C	D
E	F

Project Process and Decision Making

Projects are delivered by project teams or studios whose principals-in-charge (the closer-doers) have high degrees of involvement in project decision making. Experienced, technically oriented people provide quality-control input, but project success relies on the authority and experience of the closer-doers.

Organization Structure and Decision Making

This firm is broadly owned by professionals functioning as a partnership, whether legally structured as a partnership or as a corporation. Organization decision making is by consensus. The firm functions best when its owners share similar professional capability and goals.

Staff Recruitment and Development

This firm recruits career-oriented professionals with a strong sense of commitment to the client. Compensation consists of security via stability of practice, good benefits, and pensions but average or below-average salary. The goal is to provide security and retail experience via low turnover.

Sales Message and Type of Clients

This firm sells closer-doer experience, technical skills, and commitment to remain on top of the job with a personalized, tailored approach to the client. Its best clients are institutions and agencies with complex projects who seek reliable solutions and expect to be involved in their project's evolution. High repeat business comes from well-satisfied past clients.

Marketing Approach and Marketing Organization

Marketing relies on closer-doer principals who are strong at finding and courting clients. A facilitative marketing manager (who may be a principal) encourages broad staff participation in marketing. This firm produces a high-quality brochure and publishes a client newsletter and articles in both professional and user-oriented publications. It seeks to have a good record of awards and recognition by professional or user groups.

Pricing and Profit Strategy

Given the choice, this firm prices all its work hourly, thereby producing steady cash flow with moderate but assured profits. Even if time-and-materials contracts are not possible, it establishes its fees based on hours and costs of services. Asking for (and being worth) a higher multiplier increases profits.

Leadership and Management

In its optimum configuration, this firm has broadly based ownership with many equals. It gets by on weak leadership as long as all are committed to the goals. Consistent organization management is provided best by a facilitative general manager.

Rewards

Rewards in this firm relate to security for many in the firm—both professionally and financially in terms of benefits and growth to ownership.

Composite Type D Firm

**Strong Service
Business-Centered**

A	B
C	D
E	F

**Project Process and
Decision Making**

Projects are headed by project managers and delivered by departments whose department heads usually have authority over project decision making and responsibility for quality control.

**Organization
Structure and
Decision Making**

This firm could be a proprietorship, a closely held partnership, or a corporation with owners making decisions by majority rule. Decisions are clearly oriented toward meeting the goals of major owners.

**Staff Recruitment and
Development**

This firm hires experienced professionals as the workload requires; it seeks those comfortable in corporatelike structure. It provides higher pay but limited benefits. People at the top are entrenched; this kind of firm exhibits less loyalty to staff when workload declines.

**Sales Message and
Type of Clients**

This firm sells proven track record, demonstrably competent project managers, and strength of the organization to back them up. Its best clients are major corporations and agencies with large projects the execution of which the clients expect to delegate after making the selection.

**Marketing Approach
and Marketing
Organization**

Marketing and sales are centralized under a strong marketing director who is responsible for preparing the marketing plan. The firm will use bird dogs or prospectors to find leads, targeted direct mail, client seminars, and some advertising. Sales are closed by one or a few principals who hand off work to project managers.

Pricing and Profit Strategy

To maximize return, this firm focuses only on profitable activities, minimizes nonbillable time, carefully controls overhead, and maximizes multipliers. It can do well on lump-sum fees, hourly rates, or cost-plus fixed fee.

Leadership and Management

Owners assign strong management authority to a chief executive officer who is likely to be the most influential among them (or be the majority owner).

Rewards

This business-oriented service firm rewards the few at the top with high monetary returns.

Composite Type E Firm

Strong Idea
Practice-Centered

A	B
C	D
E	F

Project Process and Decision Making

Creative direction originates from the idea (or design) principal. Projects are delivered via highly flexible teams established and organized around jobs.

Organization Structure and Decision Making

This firm is usually owned by a sole proprietor or a few equal owners who function as partners. Their ideas and creativity in projects drive the firm, and few organization decisions are made.

Staff Recruitment and Development

Young bright professionals are attracted to this firm by its reputation and the opportunity to be associated with one of the idea leaders (gurus) of the profession. Staff members typically receive below-market salaries and minimal benefits, and they move on after a few years unless they are tapped to join the inner circle.

Sales Message and Type of Clients

The sales message is the reputation of the guru, a track record of successful innovation, and/or solutions to uncommon problems. This firm's best clients are those with unique one-of-a-kind problems or patrons with individual or corporate egos to satisfy. Clients are always the top decision makers, and they may bypass input from their organizations.

Marketing Approach and Marketing Organization

Marketing is generally unplanned. This firm relies almost entirely on a reputation developed via books, articles, professional society awards, entry in premier design competitions (often invited), frequent speeches, and often a faculty appointment. The marketing staff, if any, maintains photographic and written project information for responding to inquiries.

Pricing and Profit Strategy

Economically, this firm does best if it bases fees on the value—not the cost—of what it delivers, either by charging higher rates and multiples or high lump sums.

Leadership and Management

Strong leadership values preclude the need for structured management. The organization is led by its projects and relies on administrative support to take care of necessary tasks.

Rewards

The essential reward for this kind of firm is fame in the marketplace. Wide recognition of the importance of the ideas brings new opportunities.

Composite Type F Firm

**Strong Idea
Business-Centered**

A	B
C	D
E	F

**Project Process and
Decision Making**

Projects are delivered via stable teams or studios that often are organizaed around particular client or project types. Idea principal(s) maintain project authority.

**Organization
Structure and
Decision Making**

This firm is usually a proprietorship or small partnership (or closely held corporation functioning as a partnership). Organization decisions are tailored to maximize the application of one or a few original ideas.

**Staff Recruitment and
Development**

This firm will recruit young bright professionals interested in learning from the firm or experienced experts with records as innovators. Compensation of staff at lower levels is often below the market norm—the attraction is working on interesting projects. As staff members develop experience and want higher rewards, turnover is encouraged in order to make room for new talent.

**Sales Message and
Type of Clients**

This firm's best markets are usually clients seeking leading-edge solutions that have been successfully tested by others such as developers or lower-risk corporations, institutions, and agencies. They respond to the firm's reputation and "sizzle"—messages like "innovation that is cost-effective."

**Marketing Approach
and Marketing
Organization**

Marketing is actively planned, particularly in efforts to get to know specific clients, to seek publicity and publication of articles in leading magazines, to produce effective brochures, and so on. A marketing coordinator keeps the program moving.

Pricing and Profit Strategy

This firm strives to capitalize monetarily on the innovative ideas it develops via value-added premiums, royalties, and the like.

Leadership and Management

This firm's strong leadership is based on its ability to draw ideas and creativity from others. Management is a coordinating and administrative function.

Rewards

This firm seeks monetary rewards as well as fame. It will not consider itself successful unless it makes money as well as builds a reputation.

8

Research Findings and Self-Test

The validity of the SuperPositioning principles will ultimately be tested by the application of the principles by professionals in architecture and engineering firms. The thesis is that a firm can maximize its success—in whatever terms are appropriate to that firm—by focusing its efforts in a narrow band on the technology axis and by selecting owners who share generally the same set of values.

As a test of that notion, early in 1986 the Coxe Group surveyed by questionnaire a sample of just over 100 firms. These firms represented a mix of very small to very large staffs, were geographically dispersed, comprised different ages, had different organization formats, addressed different markets, and included most design disciplines, although predominantly architecture and engineering.

After responding to a series of questions that defined its position on the matrix, each firm was asked to rate its satisfaction with the "performance and success of the firm." ("Performance" and "success" were left to each firm to define.) Firms that reported relatively high consistency in their position on the matrix (Figure 8.1) reported relatively greater satisfaction than those who had a low consistency (Figure 8.2).

Although this sample used a brief set of questions and generally relied on one person's view of the firm, it served to confirm the essential hypothesis: Firms that have a clear notion of what they do best and how they do it best (their technology) and share a common set of goals (values) tend to enjoy the greatest success.

Self-Test

For firms interested in sampling their own consistency, a self-test is possible. The questions posed in the base questionnaire are listed in

Table 8.1. An answer page is provided in Table 8.2. To make a quick assessment of your firm's position and fit in the matrix, follow these steps:

1. Place a check mark in the answer block in Table 8.2 in response to the corresponding numbered question in Table 8.1. Ideally, there should be one answer; however, if the firm is close to being evenly divided between two or more responses, check all answers that apply.

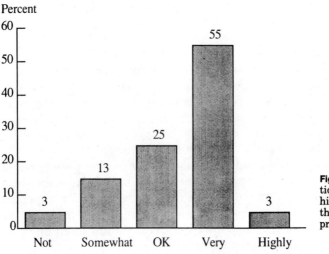

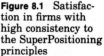

Figure 8.1 Satisfaction in firms with high consistency to the SuperPositioning principles

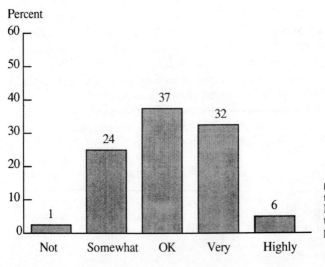

Figure 8.2 Satisfaction in firms with low consistency to the SuperPositioning principles

2. Tally the responses in each column of the answer sheet and note the totals.

3. Enter the number of responses in each cell of the matrix in Figure 8.3.

4. Note the answer(s) to question 10 to determine the level of satisfaction with the firm at its present position.

TABLE 8.1   Self-Test Questionnaire

1. Is the firm's ownership:
   a. Closely held by members of the firm acting as a partnership?
   b. Held by one or more outside investors?
   c. A broad partnership or broadly held corporation?
   d. Closely controlled internally with a corporate attitude?
   e. A proprietorship or small partnership with approximately equal ownership?
   f. A proprietorship or small partnership with unequal ownership?

2. How are firmwide decisions made?
   a. By the dictates of a professionally oriented leader.
   b. By the book, following a one-time set of rules.
   c. By consensus of the owners or managers.
   d. By the majority vote of controlling owners.
   e. Benevolently, by the leader(s) after input and collaboration of others.
   f. Autocratically, by the dictates of a business-oriented leader.

3. How do you staff?
   a. We are largely a group of highly specialized professionals with some lower-paid technical staff.
   b. We have a few professionals plus a highly trained staff of paraprofessionals able to produce most of the firm's work.
   c. We have many professionals and staff who are relatively well compensated and have been with the firm for many years.
   d. We have some specialized, high-level professionals who stay with the firm and a large technical group that turns over frequently.
   e. The brightest and best come to us; we ask a lot of them and expect that they will leave after a few years.
   f. We recruit the best and the brightest; they often leave after a few years.

4. How does the firm market?
   a. The principals sell; others do the project work; we sometimes advertise.

    b. We rely on sales representatives who are supported by advertising and competitive bidding.

    c. We have an active marketing program managed by a marketing professional. The principals participate actively by courting, closing, and being involved in projects.

    d. We organize around a centralized marketing department (PR, marketing assistance, bird-dogs, etc.). The marketing principal(s) sell(s); others largely do the project work.

    e. Our clients come to us. We publish and seek awards to maintain visibility. We succeed without a formal marketing program.

    f. Our clients come to us. We publish and seek awards; however, we have a planned marketing program.

5. How does the firm primarily organize to deliver project services and products?

    a. Departmentally.

    b. Clearly defined assembly line process.

    c. Closer-doer-led design teams or studios.

    d. Departments with project managers providing continuity on projects.

    e. Design teams brought together on an ad hoc basis.

    f. Fixed design teams or studios.

6. How are project-related decisions made?

    a. Our work is primarily the result of the standard process; design decisions are made by a lead designer.

    b. Our designs are standardized, and solutions are largely decided by the client.

    c. The project manager or closer-principal who obtains and manages the project makes the design decisions.

    d. The department head makes them.

    e. The design principal makes them; each job is consciously made different.

    f. The design principal makes them; successful solutions are often repeated.

7. What is the best route to achieve maximum rewards in your firm (however you define rewards)?

    a. High monetary rewards through maximizing efficiency.

    b. High monetary rewards through maximizing volume.

    c. Security for many—salary and benefits, profit sharing, growth to ownership.

    d. High monetary returns for a few at the top by focusing on profitable activities.

    e. Fame.

    f. Fame and fortune.

8. What is the predominant pricing system in your firm?

    a. Lump sum, getting as much as we can.

    b. Successful bidding.

    c. Hourly, with upsets.

d. Hourly, open-end.

e. Higher hourly rates and/or multiples than competitors.

f. Higher lump sums with value-added premiums.

9. How would you describe the majority of your clients?

a. Volume developers or entrepreneurs.

b. National chain clients with standardized building requirements.

c. Institutions.

d. Government or municipal.

e. Patrons in large and small organizations, and individual clients seeking unique solutions.

f. Corporations, institutions, and agencies seeking unique expertise.

10. How would you rate the overall satisfaction of the principals and staff with the performance and success of the firm? (Check one.)

Not satisfied	Somewhat satisfied	Satisfied	Very satisfied	Highly satisfied

TABLE 8.2 Self-Test Answers

Question	Responses					
	a	b	c	d	e	f
1. Ownership	[ ]	[ ]	[ ]	[ ]	[ ]	[ ]
2. Firmwide decisions	[ ]	[ ]	[ ]	[ ]	[ ]	[ ]
3. Staffing	[ ]	[ ]	[ ]	[ ]	[ ]	[ ]
4. Marketing	[ ]	[ ]	[ ]	[ ]	[ ]	[ ]
5. Project organization	[ ]	[ ]	[ ]	[ ]	[ ]	[ ]
6. Project decisions	[ ]	[ ]	[ ]	[ ]	[ ]	[ ]
7. Rewards	[ ]	[ ]	[ ]	[ ]	[ ]	[ ]
8. Pricing	[ ]	[ ]	[ ]	[ ]	[ ]	[ ]
9. Clients	[ ]	[ ]	[ ]	[ ]	[ ]	[ ]
Total						
Technology-value position	A	B	C	D	E	F

A	**B**
C	**D**
E	**A**

Figure 8.3

Analysis

A few ways to look at these data are suggested below.

Consistency of the responses, measured by the number of cells used, can indicate how well focused the firm is in its position. The ideal would be for all responses to fall into *one* cell of the matrix. (By the way, none of the respondents in the sample used just one cell.) Two or three cells are more commonly expected.

Concentration of responses can indicate the relative strength of the position. A firm using three cells and responding in a $2:1:6$ ratio is more focused and sure of itself than a firm also using three cells but responding $3:3:3$.

Contiguity is another indicator of strength. It is more reasonable for a firm to find its responses in adjacent cells (e.g., A-C) than in cells not directly connected (e.g., D-E). Also, it is more reasonable (and probably more successful) to expect adjacencies in the vertical and horizontal directions (e.g., A-B, C-E) to be more compatible than adjacencies on the diagonal (e.g., A-D, E-B). Horizontal adjacencies indicate a similar technology but a different emphasis on values. Vertical adjacencies indicate similar values but a shifting of technologies.

Multipositions may be possible. Multiple disciplines or profit centers may create more scattered results for a firm. A firm may find that these different activities have different technologies and can be effectively analyzed separately. However, the values of the total firm should be consistent in support of those technologies.

Present and future positions can be developed. Responses to the questionnaire provide a beginning for analysis. By using the descriptions of the best strategies for SuperPositioning found in Chapter 6, one can estimate the location of the firm (or profit center, etc.) on the model. That position can be described both for where the firm presently sees itself and where it feels it wants to be in the future. How to manage this shift is described in Chapter 9.

9

How to Use the
SuperPositioning Principles

Once the SuperPositioning principles are understood, the natural question is how best to apply them in managing an individual firm. As noted in Chapter 1, that depends on the circumstances.

Individuals considering the formation of new architecture or engineering firms may use the SuperPositioning principles to start their firm with greater knowledge about themselves. Established firms that are performing well in most areas may find the SuperPositioning principles helpful in identifying new ways to deal with a few issues that may seem out of place. Firms that are in transition or are experiencing general difficulties should find the principles useful both as a diagnostic tool to identify areas in the firm that may need attention and as a means of developing solutions.

The Principles as a Planning Tool

In all these cases, however, the principles offer so many choices that firms may have difficulty knowing where to start to apply them. There is a preferable sequence in the decisions that need to be made. Following this sequence may help to sort through the choices and take maximum advantage of the SuperPositioning principles.

Decide who will decide

In every professional organization, the first question that needs resolution is who will set the policies that shape the firm and its practice. Although this decision seems relatively easy when there is a single leader or the organization is a sole proprietorship, it is rarely as simple as it first appears. Consider this not infrequent example: The principal hires a new director of production (or marketing director, or technical chief) and says, in effect: "Organize your section to suit yourself." This scenario can produce considerable inconsistency unless the leader has made it clear to the person hired exactly where the firm is to be positioned and what the master strategy for the function being addressed will be.

The need for clarity in knowing the position to which the firm aspires cannot be overestimated. Whenever a firm is composed of more than a single professional practicing alone, it is essential to decide who will make that decision and how it will be made.

Few firms have a clear picture of their true position along the design technology and organization values continuums. Given the diversity of work and different project practices going on inside many design firms, no single answer is possible in many cases. It is this reason above all that has led to disappointment with so many strategic planning efforts by architecture and engineering firms.

Thus, the starting place to use the SuperPositioning principles is as a vehicle to clarify the goals of the firm.

One approach to facilitate this task in multiprincipal firms is to display the master matrix (Figure 9.1) and ask all the participants in the planning process to identify where they believe the firm is positioned at present (P) and where they would like the firm to be posi-

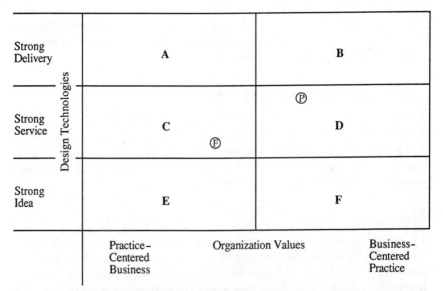

Figure 9.1 Example of goal setting with the SuperPositioning principles, where P represents the present position of the firm and F the desired future position

tioned in the future (F). Clearly, if there is consistency within it, the group can quickly move on to define the strategies to reach its goals. When there is no consistency, the exercise becomes helpful in surfacing the differences that need to be faced before the firm can expect to adopt a clear strategy.

It is at this point—when design professionals find themselves with different perceptions about the kind of practice they want to have—that the first hard choices must be faced. Sometimes, people with different initial goals can work them through to a common position that everyone will support. But it is very important to avoid a compromise that will put the firm in one of the perilous positions described in Chapter 4. When such compromising appears to be happening, the real question is whether all the participants can coexist happily in the same organization.

In these situations, the SuperPositioning principles make clear that it is not a failure of the individuals or the organization if the participants decide they will be more successful if they go their separate professional ways. The strength of successful firms flows from a common understanding among the participants about what the firm is to be. To achieve that strength, every group of professionals practicing together must ask themselves: "Are the right group of people making the decisions?"

Step one in putting the SuperPositioning principles to use is deciding who will make the required decisions.

Choose the primary technology

Once it is decided who the decision makers will be, the next step should be to define clearly the design technology that the firm will use to do its work.

The temptation may be to address organization issues first, such as whether there will be a president or managing director or whether the firm will be a partnership or corporation. But the SuperPositioning principles underscore the importance of dealing with organization structures after the choice of design technology. Technology addresses what the firm will do for its clients and how that will be done. Values shape what the firm will do for itself. Obviously, there is always some question as to which is the chicken and which the egg, but if the firm is to be successful, it must focus on what it does for clients before it addresses its own needs.

In approaching the choice of design technology, engineers and architects frequently have a very difficult time being clear about a direction. Either they resist the notion of limiting their strengths to one area or they have difficulty accepting that there is any work for which their strengths are not suited.

To sharpen one's focus, it may be helpful to think of the choices in their medical equivalents. Patients come to doctors and hospitals with a diverse range of ailments. Sometimes it's a tonsillectomy, which can be done in almost rote fashion, as on an assembly line; sometimes it's a heart attack, which needs close monitoring in the intensive care unit; and sometimes it's open heart surgery. It is not possible to serve the medical needs of all these patients in the same way and out of a single ward. Different wards (or different hospitals) specially adapted to the particular type of illness or ailment of the client are required.

Similarly, it is very difficult for any engineering or architecture organization to attempt to deal with a comparably full range of client needs. Shifting and changing project structures while trying to serve different types of client ailments is the single greatest cause of all professional firm management problems. The problem is not that there is no best way to deal with each individual "illness"; it is that each way requires very different organization and management practices.

Architects and engineers must take command of and understand the mix of their practices. Differences between well-run firms that are operated in very different ways derive as much as anything else from the fact that they are responding to very different client needs. There is not a best way to run an interior design firm. There is not a best way to run an architecture firm. There is not a best way to run an engineering firm. But there is a best way to run an engineering firm that focuses on open heart surgery–type projects. There is a best way to run an interior design firm that focuses on what might be called nursing-type projects. There is a best way to run an architecture firm that focuses on tonsillectomies.

A primary value of the SuperPositioning principles is that they highlight the difficulty of being all things to all clients. First, it is unlikely in a competitive market that any firm can be credible enough to win engagements falling all over the map. A very large professional design organization may indeed be like a hospital with separate departments and divisions handling different ailments: in effect, allowing each to evolve its own management approaches appropriate to the marketplace it serves.

That approach is illustrated by some large engineering-architecture firms that allow wide variations in various management practices between their structural, civil, and architecture divisions. As potentially divisive as this approach may sound, it is frequently a more sensible solution than attempting to impose increasingly inappropriate management practices on a firm-wide basis.

The reason why the great majority of smaller firms have difficulty settling on the best way to run themselves is that they are trying to practice in too broad a spectrum. A firm cannot be run smoothly if one day its practice is performing Strong Idea services and the next day it seeks to achieve success via efficiency from Strong Delivery services.

For many firms the course of greater wisdom is to reach for some internal consistency between its practice areas so that a single approach to management practice can be devised. Such consistency need not be absolute, but it must be sufficiently clear to provide a reasonably stable center of gravity.

In other words, a firm that is 60 percent in one design technology, 25 percent in another, and maybe 15 percent in a third, can probably resolve the various management tensions if the mix stays reasonably stable. Even though there are tensions among the different types of services, the center of balance is strong enough for management to hire the proper mix of people, adjust the pricing structure, and so on. The requirement is to keep the center stable. To vary the mix frequently will tear the firm apart and make it impossible to resolve management problems satisfactorily. When the mix becomes unstable, problems inevitably multiply.

The strongest firms of every size have a strong sense of the types of work they do best, and they organize around those types of work. That is why it makes sense to resolve the design technology question before applying organization values.

Apply the values of the leaders

The choice of design technology influences what work the firm will do; the choice of values influences the way the firm will function as an organization. Once the design technology is defined, the many decisions on how to structure the ownership, organize the marketing, manage profitability, and so on, can be made much more easily.

The issue that frequently arises when the leaders of the firm apply their values to organization problems is that the instinctive choices are frequently in conflict with the best strategies suggested by the Super-Positioning principles. When that conflict occurs, some serious soul searching about the real priorities is essential.

As an illustration, consider the real case of an architecture-engineering firm that had developed a very successful studio format for its work units, that is, its design technology. In addition to the work process, the firm had also developed an organization (values) strategy that relied on a group of associates to function as a middle-management team responsible for hiring and reviewing personnel and similar functions. The heads of all the studios were associates.

As the firm grew, it became necessary to create two new work units to expand capacity. When the principals decided to create two new studios, a serious internal conflict arose: The associates insisted that the new studios be headed by existing associates who were being transferred to the new work units. The principals wanted to promote other professionals whom they felt were qualified to head the studios and let them supervise the project work of associates in their groups. The principals felt that to allow existing associates to lead the studios simply because they had seniority and status would threaten the quality of the work. At the same time, the principals feared that violating the associate structure would discourage the middle managers.

The choice came down to a matter of client priority versus organization priority. Do we risk weakening the quality of our work or risk weakening the organization? That is a typical dilemma in design firms.

The answer according to the SuperPositioning principles is very clear. Design technology—the approach to serving clients—drives the firm. Values must be the second consideration. Otherwise, the implication is that clients don't come first.

The firm in the illustration promoted the best talent and took the temporary heat from the associates. In the end, of course, an invaluable message about the firm's priorities was sent throughout the organization. One disaffected associate did leave, but the other associates accepted the distinction between title and function and moved forward.

This example illustrates a doubly important point about applying consistent values when the time comes to promote key people to or toward the top control levels in the firm. In planning for ownership transition, it is essential that a clear decision be made about the values that are wanted and welcomed in the inner circle. Often, younger middle managers in firms represent values that contrast with rather than complement the values of the leaders. Allowing dissimilar values to rise to the top will inevitably lead to conflict and weaken the firm.

By using the SuperPositioning principles to identify and clarify issues, the leaders of the firm are better able to make the decisions that shape the firm and then communicate those decisions to others.

Staff Utilization Influences

The SuperPositioning principles also provide clear illustrations of how the work effort will be managed in the six different types of engineering and architecture firms. For example, the billable work ratio (percentage of the firm's total hours charged to clients) is different in a type B firm (in the terminology of the six positions of the matrix) than in a type E firm for comparable levels of profitability. Similarly, there is a difference in the level of marketing and sales activity required for comparable levels of work. A graphic illustration of the relative effort for firms in different positions is shown in Figure 9.2. The distribution of time is given for three levels of personnel.

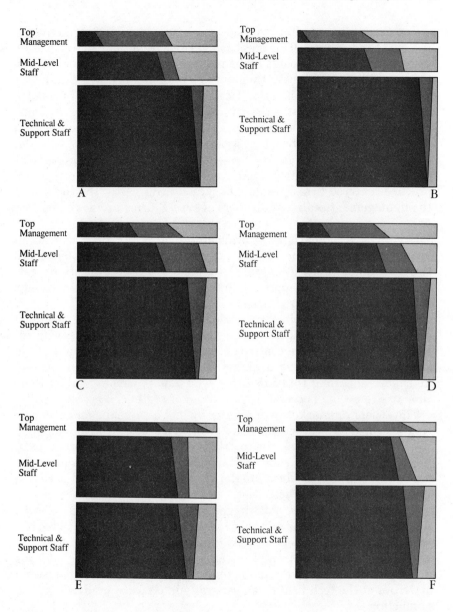

Figure 9.2 Distribution of effort among billable work, management, and marketing in the six types of firms

Key:

Billable Work
Marketing Activities
Administrative Activities

Top managers are likely to spend more time in marketing activities in type D and A firms. This emphasis springs from their role as closers who hand off work to doers. Top managers who are closer-doers in type C firms will devote more of their time to billable work while acting as hands-on involved principals. However, they will typically have a lower billable work ratio than the principals in type E or F firms, where principals put their personal stamp on each project—often from conceptual design to final project details.

Top-level managers in business-centered firms devote proportionately more time to acts of management than their counterparts in practice-centered firms. Leaders of type B firms are at the top end of the management scale, and leaders of type E firms are at the bottom end.

Side-by-side comparisons of firms at all points along the continuum show that top managers of practice-centered firms will spend more time on billable work (designing, helping solve project questions, getting into specification approval, and so on) than managers in similar roles in business-centered firms.

Mid-level managers in Strong Idea firms have a primary technical orientation and thus spend much more of their time addressing all aspects of the project conceptual solution and the nuts and bolts of the job. Thus they will have a higher billable work ratio than parallel managers in Strong Delivery firms, who tend to devote more of their time to overseeing successful application of routinized procedures.

Time spent on marketing activities by mid-level managers also varies with the firm's values. Staff members in a type C firm, for example, are likely to be following the footsteps of their closer-doer principals. They will devote more time to marketing than their colleagues in a type D firm, who will place greater reliance on central staff assigned full-time to marketing activities.

The graphs in Figure 9.2 suggest that the level of billable work among the technical and administrative staff—and the ratio of technical staff to total staff—is highest in a type B firm. That reflects the volume orientation of Strong Delivery organizations. All types of firms find it necessary to have some nonbillable time devoted to marketing activities at the technical level, generally in proposal preparation and production.

Regardless of a firm's design technology or organization values, it is axiomatic that only if the firm is well managed is there likely to be a profit at the end of each job or each year. The SuperPositioning principles make clear that there is no blanket rule about billability ratios at various staff levels of firms that will ensure profitability. Indeed, firmwide breakeven utilization ratios may vary by 8 to 10 percent between firms.

What is important to understand is that the relative proportions of staff between top level, mid-level, and technical levels vary among firm types as do the ratio of billable to nonbillable work at each level. Thus, application of average ratios derived from nationwide surveys of architecture and engineering firms may not be appropriate for all firms. Each firm's project structure, staffing mix, and profit objectives determine how billable each level of the firm should be.

Managing Hybrid Combinations

Once the managers of an architecture or engineering firm have studied the SuperPositioning principles and have determined where the firm fits on the matrix, should they expect to fit in neatly with all the strategies of a single type firm? Clearly, the answer is "unlikely." As described in Chapter 8, the higher a firm's management strategies correlate with the strategies suggested for a single sector of the matrix, the greater is the likelihood of overall success. Conversely, the more dispersed the firm's activities are among the sectors, the lower are its possibilities for overall success. That is the price of compromise. However, the degree of consistency will be relative for most firms, and the real question is how far a firm can vary from the suggested strategies and still be successful.

When a firm finds its feet planted in more than one sector, its mission is harder to define and its strategies to attain goals are more difficult to evolve. Portions of a firm's operations may be in adjacent vertical or horizontal sectors of the matrix, but the exceptions must be significantly smaller than the primary sector. Generally, the firm's staff members who work in secondary sectors do so with a higher level of frustration because they are champing at organization strategies that are essentially oriented to overall success in the primary sector.

For example, an engineering firm in which the work falls in type E, C, and A sectors in the approximate ratio of $20:60:20$ is clearly type C–dominant, and that dominance must be reflected in the firm's strategies and tactics. The principals and key staff members serving clients and carrying out work that could be better handled by a type A or E firm may evidence some discomfort with the overall project structure. The firm can expect to be successful; however, it will never know how much the dispersion among three technology sectors may diminish its ultimate performance.

In this example, the most helpful unifying factor is that all three technologies are on the practice side of the values spectrum. It would be much more difficult to design a successful management strategy for a firm with principals, work, and clients coming from sectors differing both in organization values and design technology.

Probably a common example of that circumstance would be a firm trying to manage a combination of types C, D, and B. It may have originated as a type C firm whose values have changed over the years to a combination of types C and D. Competitive pricing pressures may have been responsible for its adoption of some type B strategies to capture certain work or serve certain clients. Now internal strategy conflicts will be almost inevitable as older principals wonder what has happened to the firm they once knew "in the good old days." But these changes in the firm occurred not by conscious decision, but rather in an effort to follow work in a changing marketplace. A C-D-B combination firm is likely to exhibit internal stress and discomfort.

Firms with technology combinations, such as type E-C or D-B, are relatively common. Those that perform best clearly have a dominant type setting the rules of their game. The greater the dominance of one type the higher the likelihood for success. For example, a type C-E firm with work and clients balanced in an 80 : 20 ratio should perform demonstrably better than a C-E firm with a 55 : 45 ratio, presuming that its strategies are appropriately focused.

It can be expected also that a practice evolving from one design technology to another will perform with increasing difficulty as the new design technology intrudes. It will do so until it reaches a crossover point where the strategies required by the new design technology start to overshadow the old.

Dual combinations of technologies within design firms work better when the types share values. Thus type E-C, C-A, F-D, and D-B firms appear to have a higher likelihood for developing and implementing successful management strategies than type A-B, C-D, and E-F firms. This would be true because differences in adjacent design technology are easier to manage than differences in management and business objectives.

Firms with a dual combination of types embodying both differing values and design technologies such as type E-C-D, C-A-D, or C-D-B tend to strangle on their diversity of technologies and values, become organizationally constipated, and devote excessive time to wrestling their internal organizational problems to the detriment of service to their clients. The most practical relief will come from splitting the organization into two separate entities each with its own set of practice or business values.

Market Distribution of Firms

Empirical observations by the authors suggest that the total universe of consulting engineering and architecture firms is probably distributed as shown in Figure 9.3.

A *10 to 15%*	*8 to 12%* **B**
C *30 to 35%*	*30 to 35%* **D**
E *10 to 15%*	*2 to 6%* **F**

Figure 9.3   Distribution of professional design firms by position

Currently about two-thirds of all consulting engineering and architecture firms are primarily oriented as Strong Service design technology organizations, probably more or less equally divided between practice-centered firms and business-centered firms. As discussed in Chapter 3, this distribution is somewhat different from the current dispersion of clients along the design technology continuum, where clients are moving from Strong Service to both Strong Idea and Strong Delivery design technologies.

Firms that are trying to be responsive to the shifts in the marketplace to Strong Idea and Strong Delivery design technologies are having difficulty maximizing their strategies for success by merely adding another technology to their current makeup or beefing up an existing one. They need to recognize that they are in competition with established organizations already emphasizing the design technology they seek to add or extend. Other things being equal, the client is more likely to select the design firm with the most demonstrable strengths in the design technology sector that the client prefers.

Movement within the Matrix

A study of the histories of many architecture and consulting firms shows that most were founded by the owners with a singular position on the design technology continuum and a clear consensus (if not unanimity) on values. The passage of time and shifts in the marketplace frequently combine to move organizations from Strong Idea to Strong Service and then toward Strong Delivery.

Once a new idea becomes yesterday's idea, it is shared knowledge and enters the province of competition. The Strong Service firm frequently outperforms the Strong Idea firm and thus beats the Strong Idea firm at its own game. For a Strong Idea organization to remain firmly rooted in a Strong Idea design technology environment, it must continually replace aging ideas with new ideas. This need can be seen as the engineering and architecture equivalent of plant modernization in capital-intensive industries. Many heavy industries have learned to their owners' and employees' sorrow the price to be paid for failure to modernize their plants.

Similarly, Strong Service design organizations can remain competitive only so long as they devote adequate portions of their overall incomes to diversifying the markets in which they offer service. Once service markets become more subject to price competition, they move to the province of Strong Delivery organizations and leave the one-market Strong Service firm without clients.

Architecture and engineering firms can resist movement of their organizations along the design technology continuum by making the necessary investments in rejuvenating their markets or innovating new ideas. A conscious commitment is required to what may be classified as a form of research and development. Historically, that has not been something that many architecture and engineering organizations have seen as a needed use for their profits or capital resources. The most common migratory paths (generally unplanned) in the lives of design firms are probably those illustrated in Figure 9.3. Organization leaders can implement steps to consciously move their architecture or consulting engineering firm from one matrix sector to another adjacent vertical or horizontal sector over a period of time. A diagonal move within the matrix may be much more difficult and take longer because, in effect, it requires two moves.

Firms that start life consciously embracing type A or B strategies tend to remain wedded to their single technologies because they are positioned at an end of the continuum. These firms must be alert for the time when their specialty areas become obsolete or are taken in-house by their clients.

Radical Changes in Organization Values

When changes of organization values as firms migrate within the matrix occur slowly, they can often be absorbed with minor discomfort. However, the impact of radical changes in values, such as those that occur when engineering or architecture firms are acquired by publicly traded companies, is often very different.

The realities of investor ownership lean strongly to the dangerous extreme of Business-Centered Business (see Chapter 4). Business managers of such firms naturally emphasize financial performance because that is what their stockholders expect. Imposition of that value as the paramount criterion in a design firm's management can produce acute indigestion for the firm. Key staff members who feel their values have been short-circuited depart for more professional climes. The new owners, who often do not realize or understand the differences between their values and those of their newly acquired staff, rapidly find their acquisition to be less viable because of its loss of key people. The overnight change in organization values is most severe when practice-centered firms—especially those that have been solely or narrowly held—sell to publicly traded new owners.

The SuperPositioning principles help increase the understanding of the lack of success of the acquisitions of architecture and engineering firms by publicly and investor-owned companies. They also suggest

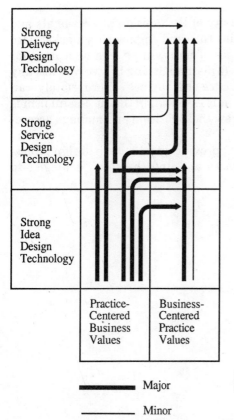

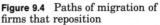 Major

——————— Minor

Figure 9.4 Paths of migration of firms that reposition

why many contemplated mergers of design firms should be approached with caution.

Principals initiating repositioning of their firms within the SuperPositioning matrix generally will find that, because of external marketplace forces, any movement against the migratory tendencies shown in Figure 9.4 will be both harder and slower to accomplish than a movement of the organization in the direction of evolution in design technology. Similarly, it appears that a move from Business-Centered Practice to a Practice-Centered Business is likewise harder to accomplish than vice versa.

Any conscious sector move within the matrix should be deliberated in depth, fully analyzed for its impact on the day-to-day and longer-term aspects of the firm's culture and life, and implemented cautiously. A behaviorally oriented observer of design firms once said: "You didn't get this way over the weekend, and you can't change yourself around to something else by next weekend."

Conclusion

Given the broad array and diversity of both design professionals and clients, there is room in the architecture and engineering marketplace for firms and practices of all types. There will always be a need for Strong Idea firms, Strong Service firms, and Strong Delivery firms, any one of which, if managed as a practice or a business appropriately, can be as successful as any other. What is essential in the successful firm is that the leading professionals know their position and manage accordingly.

The SuperPositioning principles provide a tool to help design professionals understand their differences and find the right strategies to achieve success.

Profiles of
Six Architecture Firms

The examples that follow are composite profiles assembled by the authors to describe how firms might appear if they were following the SuperPositioning principles. Any resemblance to actual architecture firms is purely coincidental.

Profile of Type A Architecture Firm

Strong Delivery
Practice-Centered

A	B
C	D
E	F

This type A firm designs office park facilities for a few developers who have discovered a certain formula for success. The architect has responded by translating the formula into planning and architectural standards and achieving success by limiting clients' options for changing the product.

Project process and decision making

Projects in the firm are processed by departments in accordance with standard details and specifications developed and refined through experience. Project decisions are made by the principal-in-charge, who has the strongest rapport with the client and the best understanding of the process and the product. Computer-aided design and drafting (CADD) is a very effective tool for this firm.

Organization structure and decision making

The firm is a proprietorship headed by the design professional, who establishes the standards for the firm's vertical structure to follow.

Leadership and management

The leader-owner sets the norms for getting the work done and also devotes extensive energy to cultivating and maintaining clients. With little time (or need) for formal management, the leader benefits from the administrative support of second-level design professionals who implement the firm's established procedures.

Staff recruitment and development

The firm is staffed with professionals committed to getting the job done efficiently. To attract the quality of staff it seeks, the firm pays above-average compensation in both salary and bonus. Job security, however, is the privilege of those at and near the top.

Sales message and type of clients

The firm's best clients are successful developers doing significant numbers of office parks and buildings. The firm sells its track record of projects that make money for its clients and its principal's knowledge of how to guide projects through local approval processes. Clients stay with the firm because of its proven product and their rapport with the principal.

Marketing approach and marketing organization

The principal sells aggressively, often by bringing new opportunities to the attention of past and current clients. The marketing coordinator keeps the name of the firm, its principal, and its office park specialty in front of past and prospective clients through public relations and direct mail campaigns.

Pricing

The firm prefers lump-sum contracts. It will bid for work with new clients as a means of getting a foot in the door, but it tries to avoid bidding on repeat work.

Rewards

Rewards for the owner are both material—the firm is accustomed to pretax profits in the 20 percent range—and personal in terms of the long-term loyalty and support of successful clients.

Profile of Type B Architecture Firm

Strong Delivery
Business-Centered

A	B
C	D
E	F

This type B firm designs and builds warehouse facilities by using tilt-up slab technology and standardized modular dimensions. Its success comes from delivering the same product over and over, not just architecturally, but via a complete design-build package.

Project and decision making

Projects are delivered by departments that are more focused than is traditional for most architecture firms. The firm divides the process into very small components. Rather than a design department and a production department, there are a wall department, a roof department, and an office department. A succession of job captains—one for each aspect of the project—facilitate the course of delivery. Each has the authority to make decisions to keep the project proceeding according to standards within a particular area. The firm makes extensive use of computerized equipment for drafting.

Organization structure and decision making

The firm is a corporation often owned by investors who are not active from day to day. Operational decision making is delegated to a chief operating officer (a senior professional), whose management authority is restricted to overseeing standard operating procedures.

Leadership and management

The owners, who originated the specialty approach to warehouses, have extensive other interests. They now look on this firm as an investment requiring little of their personal attention.

Staff recruitment and development

The extensive standardization requires less than fully trained professionals, and para-professionals are the norm. At the lower levels, staff retention is not an objective, since success comes from efficient delivery and minimal labor costs. Quality is achieved by close attention to training of new employees.

Sales message and type of clients

The firm sells standardization and reliability: an assembly line, turnkey approach. The best clients for the firm are one-time or repeat clients looking primarily at the bottom line: fast, efficient, inexpensive delivery.

Marketing approach and marketing organization

The firm's success in the market results from careful planning and management of the marketing effort. Sales representatives find and close leads. (Clients are more interested in final results; thus they will buy from others than those who deliver the work.) This particular firm gets over 70 percent of its work through price bidding. Advertising keeps the firm's name known in the market and associated with its standardized product. Heavy promotion at clients' conventions is an important marketing strategy, as is entertainment of prospective clients.

Pricing

The firm prices with low margins and accumulates profit through volume. Bidding low (but profitably) keeps volume up.

Rewards

When high volume is achieved, the monetary rewards are big for the owners-investors and senior managers who participate in profit sharing. Long-term, the owners will seek to sell the firm to others when the market is at a peak.

Profile of Type C Architecture Firm

**Strong
Practice-Centered**

A	B
C	D
E	F

This firm addresses a range of complex client and project situations. Its strength is its ability to tailor its services to the needs and styles of each client. The firm has four partner-level specialists, one dealing with health care institutions, another with laboratories, a third with prisons and correctional facilities, and a fourth with general, local practice opportunities.

Project process and decision making

Each principal specialist is a closer-doer who sells on the basis of personal ability to get the job done. A team is then assigned to each project, but the principal-in-charge retains authority over the project delivery process. The team draws on particular firm-wide technical experts as resources for specialized input in areas like specifications, estimating, and field observation.

Organization structure and decision making

With each of the closer-doers having the capability to get and guide work on his or her own, the ownership structure is four equal partners. Decision making at the organization level is shared and by consensus. A key to success is the commonality of owners' roles and goals, and the perception that all contribute equally to the firm.

Leadership and management

The firm thrives without an individual leader, since each closer-doer leads a particular market effort and the associated project delivery capability.

Staff recruitment and development

The firm historically has hired recent graduates from local and distant architecture schools, and it has a program of in-house training seminars and on-the-job learning as a means of getting people up to speed. It is committed to long-term opportunities for staff.

Sales message and type of clients

The firm's best clients are institutions and agencies whose representatives want to be closely involved in the development of the solutions. The selling points are the closer-doers' experience in tailoring the service, their technical expertise, and their commitment as "the client's architect." Eighty-five percent of its current volume is repeat or referral from clients satisfied with the rapport of the closer-doer and with the results.

Marketing organization and marketing approach

The closer-doers find, court, and sell clients, and they use the support of a marketing organization that facilitates rather than directs their efforts. The marketing staff assists by developing proposals and rehearsing team presentations. It also seeks visibility for the firm through a high-quality newsletter and award recognition; the latter is the result of a concerted effort to submit projects for consideration by clients' trade organizations.

Pricing

The firm strives to be compensated for the time it takes to deliver its projects and for the time expended in interacting with and managing the client. Hourly pricing makes the most sense, bidding the least.

Rewards

The major reward for the partners is the opportunity to be hands-on architects and take personal pride in the work that is completed. Moderate profits are divided equally among the four owners after allocation of 25 percent as bonuses to senior staff and key performers at lower levels. Future ownership opportunity for those with closer-doer capability is a major incentive for the staff.

Profile of Type D Architecture Firm

**Strong Service
Business-Centered**

A	B
C	**D**
E	F

This type D firm works on a variety of project types for corporations and developers who appreciate a well-managed delivery process and a well-managed organization.

**Project process and
decision making**

Clients' concern for a well-managed process has led the firm to focus on strong project management as the key to success. Project managers guide the project through a departmentalized structure and have responsibility for keeping the project within clients' schedules and budgets; department heads have authority over quality control and the processes within their respective departments. A difficulty has been a conflict between project managers and department heads when efforts for higher quality violate project managers' schedules and budgets. Senior owners step in periodically to arbitrate solutions.

**Organization
structure and
decision making**

The firm has a traditional, businesslike structure with six shareholders, two of whom own 40 percent each and four of whom own 5 percent each. Decisions are made with clear recognition that the power is in the hands of the majority owners, who heavily influence organization decisions.

**Leadership and
management**

One of the majority owners has been designated the chief executive officer (CEO), and he has the responsibility for directing the firm according to its business plan. Management support comes from the other owners.

Staff recruitment and development

This firm prefers to hire experienced personnel who can be immediately productive, rather than invest in training its own staff. Compensation is higher than the practice-centered competition, in part to offset lower job security (a result of not wanting to carry nonproductive staff if work slacks off).

Sales message and type of clients

The best clients for this firm are those whose own companies have similar structures. Clients expect the principals within the architecture firm to delegate day-to-day authority in the same way that they themselves do. The firm's track record, strong project management capability, and organizational strength are its best selling points.

Marketing approach and marketing organization

Centralized marketing and selling have worked well for this firm. The marketing department identifies and qualifies leads for follow-up by the senior principals, who sell. By involving the project manager in the selling process, the firm reinforces its message and begins the handoff. Public relations in the form of articles oriented to client needs and direct mail that delivers the message about the firm's ability to respond are supportive efforts.

Pricing

This firm negotiates the great majority of its work; it applies its business culture to try to weed out work that doesn't appear profitable. With close project and organization control, the firm succeeds with lump-sum contracts. Hourly pricing without upsets (not very popular with many clients) and cost-plus-fixed-fee formats are also profitable but are used in few situations.

Rewards

The firm pays high monetary returns to owners in salary and bonus, and the majority owners receive the lion's share. The reward to other partners is partly a bonus and partly the prospect of becoming majority owners.

Profile of Type E Architecture Firm

Strong Idea
Practice-Centered

A	B
C	D
E	F

This type E firm is the personal practice of a recognized master designer noted for developing unique solutions for a variety of project types. Currently the firm, with a staff of twenty-two, is designing a restaurant in Hong Kong, a waterfront housing project in San Francisco, a museum in Indiana, and an office building in Boston. The geographic range is a response to inquiries as well as the master's goal of doing projects different from those the firm has done before.

Project process and decision making

Design creativity is the most important component of the firm's success, and consequently project authority is squarely in the hands (mind) of the designer-leader. Project teams are organized to carry out the work under the direction of the leader. Project organizations are informal, and all staff members share in all tasks.

Organization structure and decision making

The firm's leader is its principal. There is little formal organization; it is projects and not the firm which interests the staff. The firm has experienced difficulties each time it has exceeded a staff size of twenty-five—its maximum has been thirty-four—because there wasn't enough of the leader to go around. The firm has an office manager responsible only in nonarchitectural areas such as accounting, scheduling, and overseeing clerical personnel. At one time the leader had a partner with similar strengths who chose to start another firm when it became apparent that the two couldn't live under one roof.

Leadership and management

The master's leadership—in design and professional goals—rather than organization management is the predominant component of success in the firm.

Staff recruitment and development

Bright, young, design-oriented professionals are attracted to the firm to work near the master. Professional satisfaction and learning opportunity are greater incentives than the level of compensation. Salaries and benefits are correspondingly lower than in other firms. Since the best younger designers don't want to work in the master's shadow once they feel they are good enough to be on their own, turnover of such people is expected. The firm has a continuing struggle to recruit and retain, at its salary scales, the technical specialists, especially in production, who are necessary resources to the design talent.

Sales message and type of clients

The design leader's reputation for innovative, exciting, and occasionally controversial buildings, often as solutions to uncommon problems, is the firm's sales message. Its best clients are those whose objectives are for unique, creative, innovative solutions and who appreciate the value of such solutions. They come from the world of patrons (e.g., a benefactor to a museum), corporations that acknowledge they have image-conscious egos to satisfy, and developers with similar objectives. The client decision maker in most cases is the individual at the top; he or she may bypass input from the rest of the organization and defer instead to the master-architect. The best clients have confidence that the buildings which result will be so exciting as to make it worthwhile to ride through the controversy that the firm's work often creates.

Marketing approach and marketing organization

Marketing is largely unplanned; the major effort is instead focused on reinforcing the firm's reputation. Books and articles whose publishers and authors seek the firm (rather than the firm seeking the opportunities) provide free publicity. Further recognition is achieved through professional society design awards, lectures, and a teaching appointment. The firm has no formal marketing staff. In lieu of one, the master's administrative assistant spends considerable time screening inquiries from prospective clients and responding to magazines and publishers interested in the firm's work.

Pricing

The firm's best clients appreciate the value of the unique solutions they will get, and the firm has learned to negotiate high lump-sum fees. It weeds out from consideration as clients those who focus initially on the prices they will pay.

Rewards

Recognition for its work—fame—is the primary motivator of the master, who, nevertheless, often belittles the accolades the work receives. He always thinks it would have been possible to do a better project. The firm has invested most of the profits it has generated on research into the influence of its work on behavior of the occupants. Consequently, the master's take-home compensation is modest.

Profile of Type F Architecture Firm

Strong Idea
Business-Centered

A	B
C	D
E	F

This type F firm recognizes the business value of innovative architecture and therefore focuses on only a few project types such that learning carries over to the next project more directly. It undertakes high-prestige developer high-rise office buildings and corporate headquarters, both of which are markets in which the owners try to outdo ("out-image") each other.

Project process and
decision making

Projects are delivered in the firm through studios co-led by a design principal and a project management principal. Both are accountable for all aspects of success on a project. Staff is permanently assigned to one studio in order to allow its members to develop the most efficient working relations.

Organization
structure and
decision making

The firm is a corporation (for tax reasons) but operates as an equal partnership of a design principal, a project–technical management principal, and a marketing-design principal. With the control of design so important, organization control is in the hands of the designer and the marketer, who understands strong design. There is a secondary level of associate principals for design and management in recognition of up-and-coming strengths that will be required for future leadership.

Leadeship and
management

The firm thrives on the ability of its leadership to nurture and harvest the ideas and creativity of its designers and apply them to its projects. Design sensitivity in managers is a key to the firm's success, since the key owners have learned that, when business goals alone predominate, design quality suffers. The business values in the firm encourage growth, which requires management attention to developing up-and-coming designers and managers.

Staff recruitment and development

The pragmatic planning of the firm leads to active recruitment and careful screening of new staff. Working on interesting projects is part of the appeal (and reward), and compensation at lower levels is often below industry averages. Turnover is encouraged for all but the very best; the firm prefers to be very selective in paying the higher salaries that go with experience and promotion. Development for those who stay continues to be on-the-job and in close proximity to the design and management principals.

Sales message and type of clients

The firm's best clients want "signature" buildings with leading-edge solutions that have been tested by others; in other words, they want to be second with good ideas but maybe first in their areas. They come from the ranks of high-visibility developers and image-conscious corporations. Such clients buy the stature and design recognition of the firm, which reflects the principals' design capabilities.

Marketing approach and organization

Principals sell to their counterparts within the clients' organization, that is, the highest-ranking decision makers. The marketing support organization actively seeks opportunities to get the firm's work published in leading magazines, since the firm benefits heavily from the visibility of its work. A four-color brochure and reprints of articles about its work in magazines are its marketing tools. A marketing coordinator keeps the overall business development program moving and researches new prospects to assure they are indeed clients for whom the firm can do its work.

Pricing

The firm, having strong business values, seeks and achieves monetary rewards as well as fame. It strives to capitalize monetarily on the innovative ideas that it develops through fat lump-sum contracts and value-added premiums. (For example: "You've targeted 15 months to 90 percent occupancy; if it reaches that level earlier, our contract stipulates that we will receive 2 percent of the gross rent above your projections.")

Rewards

The firm does not consider itself successful unless it does award-winning work and makes a lot of money. Principals benefit most from the financial success, receiving up to 150 percent of salary as bonus; associate principals receive up to 50 percent of salary as bonus; and key staff people can receive up to 25 percent.

Appendix

Profiles of
Six Engineering Firms

The examples that follow are composite profiles assembled by the authors to describe how firms might appear if they were following the SuperPositioning principles. Any resemblance to actual engineering firms is purely coincidental.

Profile of Type A Engineering Firm

Strong Delivery
Practice-Centered

A	B
C	D
E	F

This firm is successful primarily in designing short-span bridges in nearby counties. Some imagination is needed to adapt state-approved standard designs to site-specific conditions. It subcontracts with local land surveyors for mapping of bridge sites. The firm has a staff of twenty and three associates in their 30s. It is owned by two principals, one in his late 50s the other in his early 40s.

Project process and decision making

Design projects are processed through two departments, one structural and the other civil, in accordance with standard details and specifications developed by the state highway department. The structural department handles bridge design, and the civil department handles design of approach roads, utility relocation, and local street and road improvement projects. Project decisions are approved by the principal-in-charge (one of the partners), who has both client rapport and understanding of the designs that will be approved by the state highway department or owning agency. The firm uses four desktop personal computers (PCs) for engineering calculations and is investigating an integrated CADD system. Typically, the project manager is one of the two associates, who are structural engineers, on bridge work or a civil engineer associate on road and street projects.

Organization structure and decision making

The firm is incorporated primarily for tax and liability purposes. Sixty percent of the stock is owned by the senior principal, who is the president; 30 percent is owned by the other principal; and the balance is owned by two of the associates. All the associates are vice presidents.

Leadership and management

The principal is a member of a bridge advisory committee set up by the state highway department and thus is able to stay abreast of contemplated changes in standards and approval procedures. The junior principal plays a similar role with the state chapter of the American Public Works Association. The principals rely heavily on the associates to push the work along in their absence.

Staff recruitment and development

Once a year the senior principal speaks at a transportation symposium organized by the state university and relies on the exposure to attract graduate engineers to the firm. The firm pays above-average compensation in salaries and bonuses; however, it has not initiated a retirement plan. College graduates are attracted to the firm because of its solid reputation, but most of them move on after approximately three years.

Sales message and type of clients

The majority of the firm's clients are counties and cities throughout the state looking for reliable design of their projects. Clients like the technical quality of the firm's work and its familiarity with all applicable codes, standards, and the state and federal approval procedures.

Marketing approach and marketing organization

The principals are responsible for getting new work. They spend time cultivating county and city engineers at statewide meetings of their respective agencies and through other client-courting activities. The senior principal also attends symposiums organized by the American Consulting Engineers Council to keep abreast of pending changes in federal funding trends and new programs, and he uses that knowledge to alert clients early in their budget preparation process. The firm has a part-time marketing coordinator who coordinates an annual open house at Christmastime, arranges entertainment suites at county and municipal annual meetings, places tombstone advertisements in several publications, and submits news releases to local papers where projects are located.

Pricing

In most instances the firm seeks and gets lump-sum contracts except for services during the construction phase, which are on an hourly basis. Profits stem from its efficiency of delivery.

Rewards

The rewards for the owners are primarily monetary, as they are for the rest of the staff. The senior principal has been recognized in his profession by service on the state board for licensing professional engineers.

Profile of Type B Engineering Firm

**Strong Delivery
Business-Centered**

A	B
C	D
E	F

This firm depends almost totally on land development projects for less imaginative private developers building for the lower end of the housing market. It also does land surveying. It is owned by a sole proprietor, and the staff totals thirty. That includes one landscape architect who does the preliminary conceptual layout of the developments.

Project process and decision making

Initial development layouts are sketched by the planner with the primary objective of maximizing the number of housing units per acre within the code allowances. After conceptual approval by the developer, the projects are processed. Primary emphasis is on the use of standard details that have been preengineered for prior developments. The project manager, who frequently also acts as project engineer, is aware of all the county requirements for plat approval and all the utility districts' requirements for water and sewer distribution, fire protection, and lighting. All decisions are predicated primarily on keeping client costs as low as possible. A separate surveying department is responsible for site surveying and for staking out lots, building lines, grading, and utility locations. Assigned staff are mainly nonprofessionals who are trained to be familiar with the established process.

Organization structure and decision making

The owner-proprietor acts as sole decision maker on all substantive matters affecting the firm. Operating decisions are delegated to two vice presidents who are also the project managers. Recommendations for purchase of new equipment are made to the president (owner), who retains sole authority over financial decisions.

Leadership and management

The president, one vice president, the chief surveyor, and one other engineer are licensed. All other staff members are either recent college graduates or technicians. Because most technical decisions are routinized and depend mainly on known precedents, the section heads are able to make most project technical decisions without conferring extensively with the project managers. The latter's primary concerns are matters of timeliness, production, and staff scheduling and allocation.

Staff recruitment and development

Because staff retention and in-depth skills are not primary considerations of the owners, most new staff are either found by advertising in the Sunday paper or selected from walk-in applicants. Many of the technical staff can be classified as itinerant in nature; they move from firm to firm as the work load varies. The majority of the staff are paid on an hourly basis. Because wages are low, they look for maximum opportunities to do overtime work.

Sales message and type of clients

The firm's message is essentially "drive-in" engineering: "Wait a moment Mr. Client, and we'll fix your subdivision." Clients demand compliance with almost impossible deadlines, and they expect to switch projects on and off with no warning. The project managers' abilities to manage sudden fluctuations in the workload are an essential component of the firm's message.

Marketing approach and marketing organization

Most of the marketing is handled by a vice president for client relations. He has worked for several developer-oriented firms, is widely acquainted in the industry, and spends much time on the golf course with developers, realtors, mortgage lenders, materials vendors, and others who know where the next developer activity will be located. He attends all the state and local conventions and meetings of those contacts, generally entertaining extensively with a hospitality suite.

Pricing

The firm recognizes that its clients are continuously informally shopping for the lowest bid for engineering services. Most pricing is on a lump-sum basis, frequently stated as dollars per lot or other definable unit. Low price is the key to repeat client work.

Rewards

The primary monetary rewards accrue to the owner. The firm has no formal bonus or retirement program; however, in a good year the owner gives the vice presidents and the chief surveyor ad hoc bonuses.

Profile of Type C Engineering Firm

**Strong Service
Practice-Centered**

A	B
C	D
E	F

This 200-person firm has been in business over 50 years. It addresses a range of environmental, transportation, and civil engineering projects from a main office and two branch offices. There are several partner-level specialists, and each deals with a different market: one with water resources, another with dams, a third with transportation, and others with utilities, wastewater treatment, environmental pollution, and, more recently, aspects of land planning for large tracts that pose unusual engineering, community impact, and local government approval problems.

Project process and decision making

Each partner is a specialist with in-depth experience and acts as a closer-doer. Each heads a department or team and has full authority to commit the firm as to resources, timing, pricing, and so on. In the case of unusually large and/or complex projects, joint ventures, or prime-sub relationships with another engineering firm, approval of the executive committee is required.

Organization structure and decision making

The majority of the ownership is vested in the principals (though not equally, being generally skewed with seniority), and some minor ownership is spread among a number of associates. Although the firm's principals act and think like a partnership on most matters, the firm is organized as a Subchapter S corporation for liability purposes. The president, who is also the senior partner, is involved with financial matters and long-range partnership considerations, and he also acts as chairman of the board of directors (all the partners). In between board (partnership) meetings, the president heads an executive committee that primarily concerns itself with recruitment, staff training, housekeeping, and reward matters. The executive vice president is involved with the administrative support staff, billing, and spurring colleagues to collect delinquent accounts. Decision making at the board (partnership) level is shared equally even though not all principals have equal portions of ownership.

Leadership and management

Professional leadership in this firm is divided among active closer-doers and some doers who are more akin to the gurus found in a typical type E firm. Each of the support areas such as computers, personnel, and marketing is assigned to a principal who has assumed primary responsibility for its direction. Accounting and other support staff are supervised by a technical manager who has little direct input into the firm's overall management.

Sales message and type of clients

The firm's best markets are governmental agencies with complex projects for which reliable solutions are evolved from experience with analogous problems. In many instances the staffs of the state, local, and federal agencies seek to be closely involved with the development of solutions. The firm's biggest selling points are oriented around the closer-doer principal's experience, technical expertise, and commitment as the clients "consulting engineer." Many satisfied clients return to the firm on a continuing long-term service basis.

Marketing organization and marketing approach

The closer-doers find, court, and sell clients with support from a facilitative marketing coordinator who reports to one of their colleagues who acts as marketing director. The firm is still feeling its way in regard to the specific nature of the marketing director role, primarily because each principal in the past has tended to act as a Lone Ranger. The marketing staff produces high-quality brochures and a quarterly newsletter and facilitates publication of technical articles oriented toward fellow professionals. The closer-doers prefer to be active in organizations of their peers, such as the American Consulting Engineers Council, the National Society of Professional Engineers, and the Committee on Large Dams, rather than user-oriented associations. When prodded, they rather reluctantly attend organizations such as the State League of Cities or the Road Builders Association. The president, now more of a closer than a doer, gets overall visibility for the firm by serving on numerous civic, fine arts, and college advisory boards.

Pricing

Historically attuned to fees related to a percentage of a project's construction cost, the firm now prefers time-and-materials pricing plus a fixed fee with an upset maximum. At the fringes of the practice the firm is now experiencing some clients moving toward consideration of price in selection of their consulting engineer. When the firm responds to a bidding situation, it usually finds it is not the low bidder.

Rewards

Profitability is slightly above average and leads to adequate, but not huge, salaries and bonuses for all principals. Although lesser bonuses and only modest profit sharing are available for them, the rest of middle management have as their major incentives hanging in long enough and showing enough interest to become closer-doers with concommitant stature and future ownership.

Profile of Type D Engineering Firm

**Strong Service
Business-Centered**

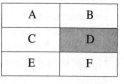

This firm has a strong business orientation and a well-developed corporate hierarchical structure. It does particularly well with clients who appreciate a well-managed delivery process from a well-managed organization. In many respects it tends to be a mirror image of the client organizations it serves. Typical clients of the firm include large public power agencies, airport authorities, and industrial clients with large manufacturing facilities.

**Project process and
decision making**

The concern of the firm's clients for a well-managed process for design of their complex projects results in the firm having a strong project manager system working in a matrix with separate-discipline department heads. The PMs keep the projects on schedule and within budget, and they are responsible for alerting the clients regarding extra work items resulting from client changes in approach or scope. The department heads are responsible for technical solutions in their aspects of the project and for quality control. Adhering to project schedules and meeting budgets sometimes conflict with the need for redesign or control of quality. In some cases, these conflicts between project managers and department heads require resolution by the division vice president.

**Organization
structure and
decision making**

With 700 employees, the firm is split into several divisions. These are generally oriented along client lines, such as power production, power distribution, airports, and

environmental pollution. Each is headed by
a senior vice president who also serves on
the firm's executive committee. Completing
the executive committee are the firm's chairman, president, and vice president of marketing. The board of directors consists of
those three plus two divisional vice presidents elected on a rotating basis. The firm is
owned by its employees through an employee stock ownership plan (ESOP). Although typically an ESOP distributes ownership in proportion to each employee's
earnings, in this case the down payment for
the ESOP was furnished by ten officers who
leveraged their ownership shares to 17 percent of the total.

**Leadership and
management**

The nature of the ESOP ownership defines
the firm's leadership. The chief executive officer (chairman) and chief operating officer
(president) were essentially self-elected at
the time of formation of the ESOP. The CEO
wields power that leads to the firm's success,
and he works closely with the COO to minimize slippage in the firm's production process and keep the machine lean.

**Sales message and
type of clients**

The firm sells a proven track record on complex projects, strong project management capability, and client responsiveness. The best
clients for the firm are those who relate well
to the corporate mentality and who delegate
their project management downward to
their consulting engineer's opposite number.
Thus the firm relies on multilevel liaison
with its clients at the chief executive, group
vice president, and project manager levels.

**Marketing approach
and marketing
organization**

The firm has a centralized marketing department whose head coordinates closely
with the marketing manager assigned to
each division. All marketers are trained engineering professionals who can speak a
prospect's language and orchestrate their di-

vision's courtship of the prospect. They know when to involve the division vice president, when to display the expertise of a technical expert, and when and how the top executives should be involved. Senior project managers, division vice presidents, and top executive officers are involved in user group associations. The central marketing office facilitates production of responses to requests for proposals (RFPs), orchestrates client-oriented technical seminars on emerging areas of particular interest, and produces targeted direct mail.

Pricing

The firm will work on a cost-plus-fixed-fee basis, but it is happier with lump-sum contracts; its businesslike approach makes it possible for such contracts to maximize profits. Thus, the best clients are large organizations able to fully define the scope of work.

Rewards

The firm pays its top officers reasonably well, but in lieu of large bonuses it is currently paying off debts assumed to finance the ESOP. This gives the top officers steadily greater equity to be drawn at retirement.

Profile of Type E Engineering Firm

**Strong Idea
Practice-Centered**

A	B
C	D
E	F

This is a fifty-person firm specializing in un-usual aspects of environmental pollution, particularly wastewater treatment involv-ing removal of exotic pollutants that are typically nonresponsive to normal primary and secondary wastewater treatment. The founder is widely acclaimed as the origina-tor of some of the successful treatment methodologies now used to treat unusual trace pollutants.

**Project process and
decision making**

Because prospective clients have heard of the founder's fame, they solicit his direct in-volvement to help solve their unusual prob-lems. Project teams are organized around this guru, and key assistants typically have one or two graduate degrees. (The firm has an unusually high proportion of PhDs on its staff.) Project decision making is approached on a quasi-team basis, always looking for the guru's approval before finally moving to-ward implementation. The client expects the guru to be involved in presentations at key points during the project, and that has the effect of limiting the firm's size.

**Organization
structure and
decision making**

The firm is a sole proprietorship; it is incor-porated only for tax and liability purposes. As such, all consequential decisions are vested in the founder-owner. Nontechnical and housekeeping decisions are left to a gen-eral office manager. Two long-time col-leagues have long since reconciled them-selves to the classical roles of aides-de-camp. They are free to give their opinions on matters to the owner, and he feels equally free to ignore them.

Leadership and management

There is one leader of the firm. Others who come closest to exercising any real management responsibilities are primarily involved in staff support activities such as accounting, scheduling, computer management, and overseeing clerical personnel.

Staff recruitment and development

Because the firm's leader speaks frequently at engineering graduate schools and is widely published in the technical literature, the name of the firm is well known to the brightest environmental engineering graduate students. This assures the firm of a steady stream of volunteered résumés. Engineering colleagues in academia also steer their top-line doctoral students to the firm for summer intern work, which frequently leads to full-time positions on graduation. Salaries and benefits are lower than in other firms. Employees place much higher emphasis on the professional experience gained from working closely with an industry leader.

Sales message and type of clients

The majority of the firm's clients have very special one-of-a-kind pollution problems for which innovative solutions are necessary. Often, a large share of its clients are other service-oriented engineering firms who may realize they have bitten off technically more than they can chew and call on the guru for help or who are competing for assignments with an unusual pollution component. Other clients may be project owners who are encountering difficulties in resolving a problem with their day-to-day consultants. In all events, the guru's reputation is the sales message and the selection determinant.

Marketing approach and marketing organization

Primarily, marketing results from marketplace exposure arising from technical articles, textbooks, and guest lectures before technical groups and at academic institutions. Several projects on which the guru worked have been recognized by awards from the American Society of Civil Engineers, the American Consulting Engineers Council, and the Water Pollution Control Federation. A marketing coordinator helps respond to inquiries, sends reprints of technical papers, and facilitates preparation of articles for technical journals and other print media.

Pricing

Because the scope of work is often inexact or hard to define, the firm works primarily on an hourly basis at rates well above average for the engineering profession. Prospective clients who attempt to nail down costs to specific amounts before work begins do not have much currency at the firm.

Rewards

The primary motivator for all but the founder is the reflected glory that comes from working with a guru. The founder receives both personal recognition and well above average recompense.

Profile of Type F Engineering Firm

**Strong Idea
Business-Centered**

A	B
C	D
E	F

This firm recognizes the business value of innovative engineering solutions to industrial hazardous waste problems. It also knows that innovation for innovation's sake can be deleterious to profit, so it keeps its focus narrowed so learning can carry over directly to analogous situations. The firm has a staff of 100 and has established several branch offices strategically located to serve potential clients and to provide prompt response to waste spill situations.

**Project process and
decision making**

Projects are handled in the firm by specialist-led project teams each of which handles a specific type of waste problem. The branch offices are, in effect, small permanent project teams that can call upon the total engineering and scientific resources of the firm for problems that are more intricate than their local expertise can handle. This works well because the firm is dedicated to strict avoidance of the "not invented here" syndrome. Giving the firm's clients its best solution to each problem enhances its marketplace position, and coincidently, its bottom-line profit.

**Organization
structure
and decision making**

Although organized as a corporation to help protect the owners against liability exposure and to focus better on profitability, the firm is, in effect, a series of interlocking partnerships of the (founding) partnership at the head office and junior partnerships at the branch offices. A first-generation firm, organization decisions are made by the president with input from other "founding partners" and branch office managers whose views are particularly respected. Decisions ensure that the firm keeps to its chosen narrow sector of the engineering marketplace.

Leadership and management

The firm's leaders recognize that they are operating in an uncharted market and that their market leadership will be assured only as long as they devise innovative and cost-effective solutions for their clients' problems. The firm thrives on the president's ability to attract bright, entrepreneurial department heads and branch office managers by giving them their heads in evolving innovative solutions to very challenging problems.

Staff recruitment and development

The firm pragmatically concentrates on recruitment of known bright performers in the environmental engineering marketplace. Young engineers join the firm because of the appeal of working at the cutting edge under the leadership of senior principals who are rapidly becoming recognized for their innovations. The fast pace of activity and long hours ensure that only the brightest and toughest stay for the longer term and the higher rewards. For those who stay, the firm supports extracurricular short-course and higher-education training.

Sales message and type of clients

Because of the nature of their hazardous waste problems, the firm's clients cannot afford adverse publicity resulting from engineering failure. There is, therefore, a strong tendency for the firm's clients to shy away from being the first to try new treatment approaches, but they are more than willing to be second in the marketplace to apply what are essentially debugged innovations or more assured solutions. Thus the firm concentrates on selling its record for performance: perfect solutions to tough problem situations. In effect, the firm tells prospects,

"We know what will work for you, and we know how to modify solution X that was tried in situation Y so it will work better for you."

Marketing approach and organization

Principals sell to their counterparts in industry and in key government agencies, that is, to the president, plant manager, or highest-ranking decision maker. The firm concentrates on getting its work published either in leading user-oriented magazines or as papers written by senior principals for presentation at professional engineering symposiums oriented toward audiences concerned with hazardous waste problems. From time to time the firm sponsors in-house seminars, to which clients and prospects are invited, as vehicles for displaying the staff's expertise. The firm publishes a newsletter three times a year with stories highlighting its solutions to clients' problems. A marketing coordinator keeps the program moving and maintains extensive mailing lists segregated by client type, location, and so forth.

Pricing

The firm seeks lump-sum contracts or time-and-materials contracts with above-average multipliers. Because many of the key staff are emerging leaders in their respective fields, their salaries are high, and thus hourly rates also are high. The firm is able to claim a premium for its ability and its willingness to respond instantly to spill problems.

Rewards

A key element of the president's and the firm's striving for success is high monetary reward as well as building a reputation as a leader in the field of hazardous waste. The founding owners, senior principals, and branch office managers benefit most from the firm's financial success.

Profiles of Six
Interior Design Firms

The examples that follow are composite profiles assembled by the authors to describe how firms might appear if they were following the SuperPositioning principles. Any resemblance to actual interior design firms is purely coincidental.

Profile of Type A Interior Design Firm

Strong Delivery
Practice-Centered

A	B
C	D
E	F

This firm focuses on interiors of proprietory hospitals, for which it has found "a concept" to which a small body of repeating clients respond. It has a staff of twenty-eight, and it is tempted to, but thus far has shied away from, becoming a contract interiors firm.

Project process and decision making

The interior designer who owns the firm has defined the concept for the specialty, proprietary hospital interiors, and is the ultimate decision maker for the three project teams. The defined standards minimize the number of project decisions that reach the owner's level. CADD has proved effective for the firm for both its graphic application and its ability to specify wall finishes, ceilings, carpentry, and furnishings. These applications increase the efficiency and comprehensiveness of its documents package, benefits for which it is well known in the marketplace.

Organization structure and decision making

The success of the firm is clearly tied to its ability to respond to its clients quickly and inexpensively through central control in the proprietor's hands. The proprietor is solely responsible for decisions relative to external issues—how are needs of the market and our current clients changing?—and draws input from senior technical staff.

Leadership and management

A component of the firm's success is the confidence its professional staff has in the judgment of the leader-owner. Second-line management is composed of professionally trained and experienced project managers who accept the leader's direction, understand the delivery-related success criteria—efficiency and technical quality—and work diligently to keep work to, not above and not below, the defined standards. The health care conglomerates' projects are in various parts of the country. With one office location (to satisfy the client's concerns for consistency), the firm's project managers are often on the road, especially during construction and installation.

Staff recruitment and development

The owner recognizes that experienced personnel at all levels make life easier and more profitable. Consequently, the firm relies heavily on three project managers who are compensated above industry average for their responsibilities. They in turn supervise low-level personnel, who although professionally trained, are inexperienced, inexpensive, and energetic. Personnel development is task- and short-term-related; it is focused on standards and techniques. The majority of the lower staff members expect to move on within two years when they learn the ropes.

Sales message and type of clients

The firm delivers the message to its past and current clients that it knows when to incrementally adjust its formula to assure patient-user appeal while always focusing on efficient delivery and problem-free results. Its clients, forever busy finding the next site and structuring the next deal, are delighted with the firm's ability to get interiors finished satisfactorily with little input and monitoring from the conglomerates' development staffs.

Marketing approach and marketing organization

The owner maintains personal rapport with the development division head in each of the clients' organizations. Through trade journals, health care conferences, and so on, the principal maintains a keen awareness of trends in the market. Friendships are developed within appropriate networks and by entertainment aboard the owner's 43-foot ketch. The proprietor is careful to avoid serving competing clients, and his concern for clients' proprietary rights has created a degree of client loyalty.

Pricing

Experience and resulting efficiency allow the firm to quote lump-sum fees for its work. After early bidding for each of its major clients, it has achieved a position such that the price is generally received and accepted. The onus is on the project manager to deliver, and on occasion the owner has accepted cost overruns rather than provide reason for clients to question the firm's efficiency and its ability to control its work.

Rewards

As with type A firms in other fields, high monetary return accrues to the owner, who shares a small amount of that with senior staff. There is a secondary satisfaction: the fact that several clients, all of whom see monetary return as their keys to satisfying lives, have become true friends with common nonbusiness interests.

Profile of Type B Interior Design Firm

Strong Delivery
Business Centered

A	B
C	D
E	F

This firm is a wholly owned subsidiary of a furniture dealership that delivers branch banks finished completely, starting with an empty shell and ending with handing out logo-inscribed key chains. "Contract interiors," including design documentation, purchasing, and installation, all with a turnkey approach, are the firm's strength. The staff size is sixty-two.

Project process and
decision making

Senior project managers guide work through the several departments that make up the assembly line approach—space planning, color selection, furniture and cabinetry specifications, graphic design, purchasing, and installation. Department heads monitor the delivery process. Project managers contract with department heads for schedules and budgets for their respective portions of the work.

Organization
structure and
decision making

The numerous departments of the delivery process define the organization structure. A general manager, hired by the parent company, has management authority. The general manager gets frequent input from project managers and department heads and has bottom-line responsibility measured in billings, profit, and return on investment. (The latter permits comparison with other entities under the parent's ownership.)

Leadership and
management

The parent company spun this entity off as a subsidiary when it became clear that, with a good product and a standardized approach to delivery, hands-on leadership and management by the founding owners was no longer necessary. The general manager and the project managers accepted the opportunity to run the business, and they share in the profits as long as extensive input and new working capital are not required from the parent. To date this approach has been effective, in part because of the success of its commission-earning sales force.

Staff recruitment and development

It is clear that the major staff components for success in this firm are (1) effective salespeople, (2) experienced project managers, and (3) a low-cost production group. Since the standard approach requires only basic skills, low-paid paraprofessionals fill the lower ranks. It is the process rather than the staff that receives most of management's attention. Salespeople are paid via commissions, and other senior staff are paid salaries plus profit shares. Minimal attention is given to staff development, since at lower levels the skills are easy to acquire and at senior levels the firm tries to hire the experience and skills it needs.

Sales message and type of clients

The best clients for the firm are smaller banks in midsize metropolitan areas (populations up to 1 million) who seek fast, trouble-free turnkey delivery. The average bank client opens one new branch per year, generally in an office building or shopping center.

Marketing approach and organization

The marketing manager, with the general manager, plans activities that keep the firm in tune with the banking industry and abreast of local market demographics and expansion plans. Display at trade conventions provide good exposure and new leads. Four sales representatives, working geographically, handle house accounts.

Pricing

Fixed prices pave the road to success. After initially working closely with project managers, salespeople have learned to price both competitively and profitably. Profitability increased when the sales commission structure was changed. It is now half based on fee and half based on project profit.

Rewards

Salespeople and managers have specific financial rewards in addition to salary. The parent company is rewarded largely by profits and by the broader stability that diversification provides. The parent currently receives 65 percent of subsidiary profits, and the remainder is distributed to senior staff. (The decision has already been made that if the market appears saturated, if profits show a steady decline for three consecutive years, and if the return on investment falls below the prime interest rate for three consecutive years, the parent will actively try to sell the firm.)

Profile of Type C Interior Design Firm

**Strong Service
Practice-Centered**

A	B
C	D
E	F

This firm has a staff of forty-two divided into three groups: one serving corporate clients, another handling (via CADD) facilities management for any type of clients, a third, also using CADD, doing tenant space planning for several developer clients with whom the firm has continuing open-ended contracts.

Project process and decision making

The leaders of each of the groups, which are in fact studios, have total responsibility for project completion and accountability for budgets and schedules. Each partner-leader has the last word on all project decisions. CADD is used in the facilities management and tenant planning studios, where constant base information and design repetition mesh well with capability.

Organization structure and decision making

The firm's organization structure is a direct consequence of its project delivery system. The three studio leaders-partners and a fourth managing partner make decisions by consensus, although within each studio, the partner-leader has high authority.

Leadership and management

With three partners being heavily project-, client-, and studio-oriented, it is the fourth to whom overall firm management has been delegated. The managing partner is responsible for overseeing the firm's marketing and financial activities and for facilitating dialogue among all partners toward planning and policy decisions.

Staff recruitment and development

The firm prides itself on low turnover and the willingness with which partners and senior staff accepted salary reductions during the most recent recession in order to be able to keep the majority of its personnel whose contributions toward client satisfaction are important. This commitment to staff retention is reflected in an in-house training program, which is necessary because the teams are composed of generalists who must learn broad skills.

Sales message and type of clients

The sales message of the firm is: "We have a group dedicated to each of the markets we serve; and when you retain us, you also retain a partner-expert who heads the group undertaking your project." The best clients are repeat clients. That is mandatory in the facilities management and tenant studios because, without expectation of repeat work, the start-up efforts are not justified in either energy or cost.

Marketing approach and marketing organization

Partners who lead studios maintain close rapport with their clients. A marketing coordinator, who has good writing skills, assists in preparing proposals that studio leaders submit. Generally it is the track record of satisfied clients that gives credibility to the sales message. A quarterly newsletter is intended to keep all clients and the markets aware of the firm's strengths.

Pricing

The firm has an interesting pricing dichotomy: the corporate studio prices by hourly fees and the other two studios price on a unit basis. That is, a price per square foot is negotiated initially, and it becomes the basis of compensation for facilities management and tenant work.

Rewards

Having been willing to make personal financial sacrifices during lean periods, the partners themselves share much of the pie during good years. Senior staff members receive respectable bonuses, and more modest bonuses are distributed to lower-level personnel whose performance is noteworthy. Job security is an important reward to all personnel.

Profile of Type D Interior Design Firm

**Strong Service
Business-Centered**

A	B
C	D
E	F

Type D firms can become quite large compared to the rest of the interiors profession. This firm has a staff of 160, three senior partners, and six junior partners. The firm is divisionalized by specialty. Its interior divisions direct their services to the institutional market and the corporate market; a recently added architecture division has been successful in creating an identity in restoration and renovation work. In addition, the firm has a small division dedicated to graphic design, primarily for corporate and institutional clients and often where another division is already involved. Two branch offices, each replicating one division of the head office, have staffs of twenty and sixteen.

**Project process and
decision making**

Divisions are coheaded by junior partners, each having a mentor at the senior partner level. One of the coleaders is design-oriented, the other is management-oriented, and both are accountable for division performance. Within each division are project teams composed of specialists—designers and technicians—who report to a dual leadership, generally a project designer and a project manager. Budget constraints on smaller projects limit leadership to one person, generally called a project manager. Project leaders are responsible for project success, and budget and schedule objectives are defined by division leaders.

**Organization
structure and
decision making**

The firm's structure has essentially three tiers. At the highest level are the three senior partners, who address such overall issues as strategic planning, financial performance, and maintaining rapport with their peers in client organizations. They have chosen to remove themselves from all but the most cursory overview aspects of project delivery. In expanding ownership, the senior partners identified individuals with particular strengths—design or project management, for example—rather than having the range of strengths that the senior partners see in themselves.

Leadership and management

Overall, the nine partners meet quarterly. Major decisions are made by vote of shares, since the senior partners hold 72 percent of the ownership and their influence on the firm is substantial.

Staff recruitment and development

A personnel office routinely scans other divisions' anticipated excess staff. If needs can not be filled by this route, the personnel office undertakes targeted recruiting and staffing. Many staff are recruited from other interiors firms, although a significant percentage joins the firm without prior job experience. Training, particularly in working within the firm's coheaded team structure, has been important in bringing people up to speed quickly. Training has also been valuable in getting high utilization and benefits from such in-house resources as the library, the CADD system, and the reprographics department. In-house seminars help in maintaining awareness of new furniture and products on the market.

Sales message and type of clients

The message of the firm is exemplified in its project leadership: a business approach (via project manager) to good service and design (via project designer). Clients most responsive to this message are large institutions, Fortune 500 corporations with constantly changing space needs, and a few developers active in renovation work within the urban core.

Marketing approach and marketing organization

The firm's marketing approach is based heavily on the senior partners' ability to gain referrals from one large client to the next. Junior partners get heavily involved in proposals, fee negotiations, and assignment of staff into project teams. An expensive brochure is redone every two to three years and sent to all past and current clients with a personal note from one of the partners. The marketing staff, composed of a marketing manager, a marketing coordinator, a technical writer, and a secretary, works for one senior partner who has been designated as marketing director.

Pricing

The firm's pricing reflects its business sophistication. Contracts are hourly with high multipliers (quite profitable when several alternative schemes and furnishing systems are thoroughly explored and the efforts to do so are billed) or a percentage of estimated construction and furnishings costs.

Rewards

Diligence to financial monitoring has made the firm very profitable. Senior partners benefit the most with bonuses of up to 150 percent of salary, and junior partners also do well, earning as much as 75 percent of salary as bonus.

Profile of Type E Interior Design Firm

Strong Idea
Practice-Centered

A	B
C	D
E	F

This firm has a single, internationally recognized designer as its owner. Clients see the designer's work published in professional and trade journals, and the designer's name is attached to products which are marketed and distributed by a major manufacturer. Current work includes headquarters office facilities in Europe and several corporate and hospitality facilities in the United States. With a staff of seventeen the firm does all its work from one office location.

Project process and decision making

Projects are organized around the designer-owner, and much of the staff is simultaneously involved with more than one project team. The designer-owner makes the decisions. The project process emphasizes many alternative design and redesign studies, and fat fees make that feasible.

Organization structure and decision making

The autocratic style of the designer is dominant. Others on the staff assume some responsibilities when certain issues seemed to receive inadequate attention, yet the designer steps in and overrules frequently. A business partner is relatively low in the office hierarchy, having chosen to retreat after being similarly overruled many times.

Leadership and management

The designer and the projects lead. All others follow. No one manages. The firm is small enough that management roles per se are unnecessary.

Sales message and type of clients

The message is the high-design impact of the firm's work. The best clients are image-conscious corporations who typically seek one-of-a-kind treatments for their corporate headquarters. A secondary client is the furniture manufacturer for whom the designer has created several additions at the high price end of its product line.

Marketing approach and marketing organization

The firm's marketing approach consists of maintaining rapport with the publishers of the right magazines and journals. There is no marketing organization. The designer personally follows up on inquiries and establishes new contacts via business and social circles.

Pricing

Hiring this firm is an expensive proposition both in fee (high multiple or lump sum) and in expenses (the designer is absorbed in a life style that clients are expected to support via first-class travel and so on).

Rewards

Recognition is a reward for all in the firm; it comes in the form of professional awards as well as extensive publication. Financial reward beyond salary is primarily the domain of the designer-owner, although some bonus compensation is allocated to staff.

Profile of Type F Interior Design Firm

**Strong Idea
Business-Centered**

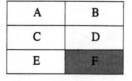

A	B
C	D
E	**F**

This firm has two owners, both of whom are design-competent and business-aware (one more business-knowledgeable than the other), and two specialties: professional offices and graphic design for a range of client types. One of the principals is a woman. Ownership is skewed slightly in her favor so the firm can qualify as a woman-owned business enterprise.

Project process and decision making

There are four semipermanent teams, each headed by a designer who reports to a principal-in-charge. Typically, project decisions are made by agreement between the owners; but on issues particularly important to either principal, he or she prevails.

Organization structure and decision making

The structure is clearly hierarchical, although the principals solicit input from senior staff and are always open to it. Once major decisions are reached, implementation decisions are made with those who will be involved.

Leadership and management

The leadership values of the principals guide the firm; key staff whose understanding of these values is evident are given project and some organizational responsibility. When time conflicts arise, client-project issues come first despite the business values of the firm.

Sales message and type of clients

The firm has finally been able to impress on certain clients and prospects that there is value to high design and that this value exceeds its cost. The firm's own office is glowing testimony to this, and the best clients are those who see the firm's work and understand the value of the investment. Although graphic design fees per project are considerably lower, the same message is communicated.

Marketing approach and organization

A principal is designated for and active with every client. A newsletter showing current work keeps the firm's message in front of past clients. Seeking periodic feedback from past and current clients through "focus groups" and informal discussions helps the firm stay aware of its image and the images of its competition. A strong aspect of its marketing is simply getting prospects into its office to experience its high-design approach in its own facilities.

Pricing

The firm's greatest success comes with lump-sum contracts. Recently, as service firms have attempted to increase their presence in the firm's markets, it has agreed to hour-based compensation from some clients, but with a higher multiplier.

Rewards

Although the profits are there, most have been left in the firm in the form of facilities. Principals and senior staff now look forward to profit distribution. Recognition—being published and awarded—is a reward for all.

Index

Index

ABOUT THE AUTHORS

Weld Coxe, Nina F. Hartung, Hugh Hochberg, Brian J. Lewis, P.E., Robert F. Mattox, FAIA, and Peter A. Piven, FAIA, are principals of The Coxe Group, Inc., Philadelphia, the largest consulting organization in the United States specializing exclusively in the management of architectural, engineering, interior design, landscape architecture, planning, and other professional design firms. David H. Maister is principal of his own management consulting firm, Maister Associates, in Boston.

WELD COXE, founding principal, studied at Harvard College and became active in the design community in 1960. He is the author of *Managing Architectural and Engineering Practice* (Van Nostrand Reinhold, 1982) and *Marketing Architectural and Engineering Services* (Van Nostrand Reinhold, second edition, 1982). He is a certified member of the Institute of Management Consultants and a charter member of the Professional Services Management Association and the Society for Marketing Professional Services. Mr. Coxe was elected an Honorary Member of the American Institute of Architects in 1976.

NINA F. HARTUNG is a specialist in human resources management. She is a graduate of Marietta College and received advanced training at the Cornell School of Labor and Industrial Relations, the University of Pennsylvania, and the American Management Association. A member of the American Society of Personnel Administrators, Ms. Hartung regularly conducts seminars on personnel matters.

HUGH HOCHBERG, a graduate of Rensselaer Polytechnic Institute and the Harvard Business School, focuses his consulting efforts on issues of organization structure, marketing, ownership transition, and management. He is the author of the chapter "Business Organization and Management" for the *Handbook of the American Institute of Architects*, and he has conducted management seminars in the United States, Canada, and Australia.

BRIAN J. LEWIS, P.E., a graduate of the University of Durham (U.K.) and UCLA, founded and managed his own successful consulting engineering firm in the state of Washington and subsequently served as marketing director and president of one of America's largest environmental engineering firms. He has been active in Chapters and National Committees of the American Consulting Engineers Council for over 20 years, and he has authored numerous technical articles on design firm management. Mr. Lewis has conducted management workshops in the United States, Great Britain, Pakistan, and New Zealand.

ROBERT F. MATTOX, FAIA, is an architect (Rice University) and earned a masters in business administration from the University of Michigan. He has specialized in developing computer tools for design practice and has served as general manager of firms in Michigan and Iowa and as vice president of a firm in San Francisco. Mr. Mattox is the author of *Financial Management for Architects* (American Institute of Architects, 1980) and the revised AIA book, *Standardized Accounting for Architects*.

PETER A. PIVEN, FAIA, holds degrees from Colgate, the University of Pennsylvania, and Columbia University and is a specialist in architecture firm management. He was first chairman of the Financial Management Task Force of the American Institute of Architects, and he is the author of "Financial Management" in *Current Techniques in Architectural Practice* (American Institute of Architects, 1975) and *Compensation Management: A Guideline for Small Firms* (American Institute of Architects, 1982).

DAVID H. MAISTER is principal of *Maister Associates, Inc.*, a Boston-based consulting firm specializing in the management of professional service firms. Educated at the University of Birmingham and the London School of Economics, he earned a doctorate in business administration from the Harvard Business School, where he served as Associate Professor until 1985. Dr. Maister has been a consultant to leading firms in a variety of professions including accounting, law, health care, investment banking, and public relations, and he has had numerous articles published in professional journals.